D1715768

MULTIFAMILY REAL ESTATE INVESTING

How to Achieve Financial Freedom by Investing In Multifamily Real Estate

FRANCIS MUSAU (CIMA, CeMAP)

Here's A Gift For You!

Buying real estate is a big financial commitment, so you should also be investing some time in making sure you know what you're buying and that you're getting a fair deal. This made easy guide covers everything you need to know about due diligence.

SCAN HERE TO CLAIM YOUR COPY!

Visit us:

www.fmusau.com/free-gifts

CONTENTS

INTRODUCTION

As economic crisis and recession subside, it is high time to dust ourselves off and look to the future. Americans are resuming their lives and making new plans, using the lessons they have learned in the past few decades.

The recent years have changed our priorities, as well as behavior moving forward. Companies and businesses, big or small, are not only restructuring but also considering new directions and strategies to make profits. This new approach will help bring employees together to create a new culture.

Interestingly, the changes are particularly relevant and applicable to family businesses that typically merge business and personal goals. When it comes to a real estate family business, it is intertwined with family dynamics.

These dynamics may continue to impact new cultural patterns and demands for commercial and residential space, areas of risk, migration trends, and, most importantly, opportunities in real estate investing.

It is important to remember that the financial and behavioral fallout affects each market differently, building, and property type.

As such, every real estate family business can experience a different set of risks and challenges. Considering this, it is perhaps the right time to learn how investing in a family business can benefit you, which types of small multi-family can turn into the best rental properties. You should also know what you need to assess in your multi-family investment property and methods to create a million dollars in net.

If you're a family leader and looking for guidance and ways to get your business off the ground, understanding the real estate family business to its core is CRUCIAL to preserve cash value and assets. Rethinking your family business matters in the real estate environment can be the right step to take to reduce financial strain. This is because it can provide you with more focus.

Family business, as the title suggests, is actively owned, managed, and operated by family members. The single-family members hold a major percentage of business ownership. They have control over strategic decisions. In fact, either it can be the involvement of more than one generation of a family or has senior management of the business from the same family.

In real estate, a family business comprises family properties, such as storage units, family homes, multi-family properties, and buildings. A family-owned business is usually controlled by a family member or the entire family. This controlling ownership enables the family to create and decide on the business objectives, strategies, and policies.

Note that family businesses or companies in the real estate industry control a great portion of the property market. This may sound strange, but most family businesses in this industry not only outperform non-family businesses but also last longer.

Whether the main focus of a family business is on construction, financing, development, or any other subset therein, it is substantially important to have a deeper understanding of how you can keep it afloat from generation to generation and maximize revenues.

Moreover, if it is the first time you're planning to invest in a real estate business, you need to learn the characteristics of a successful real estate business. Knowing how you can structure and organize your real estate business can make a world of difference.

People who manage or work for a business in the real estate industry can learn from this book. Precisely, you can find out how to invest in real estate property.

BUT before we plunge into this discussion, let's quickly understand the types of real estate family businesses and why investing in these businesses is the right idea.

Single Family Business (SMB) – We classify single-family real estate investing as a business that includes only one unit. Many people start as single family investors as they consider it a more affordable option. However, cash flow is not as strong unless one owns many multiple properties.

One key area in an SMB is "investment management." It may include establishing investment criteria and then making investments according to that criteria.

Keep in mind that it may take plenty of different forms. The investment in one single unit, subsequently, must be risk-managed and controlled. Related tasks also need consideration. These tasks include regular report preparation and understanding different tax aspects of running a family business.

It is important to research the right property or unit to invest in. Investors expand the search outside their local area. In fact, many investors prefer investing in single-family units outside their states. It is because in some housing markets, properties cost thousands of dollars.

Real estate is one of the popular domains when it comes to investing in singly family businesses. It is because it has steady and stable dividends. Plus, the assets and money invested are more consistent and stable than shares.

Some SMBs in the property industry hire an investment team or specialize in private equity. However, other businesses rely on external property managers.

Why Set up a Single-Family Business

One prerequisite for establishing a single-family business is that you have sufficient assets. Also, some basic reasons why family businesses are formed are as follows:

- Generation change: The last generation has left the family business- the assets need to be handed over to the current generation in an orderly manner.
- Property ownership: The family owns considerable land. The establishment of the single-family business will monetize and expand the portfolio.
- Professionalization: By founding the family business, the investment is professionalized and organized.

Multi-family Business (MFB) - Unlike single-family businesses in real estate, a multifamily business refers to owning a "multifamily property or MDU (multiunit dwelling). It can be a residential building with more than two properties under one roof. Or it can also be many buildings within a single complex.

Multifamily houses typically comprise apartments, townhouses, duplexes, condos, and quadruplexes. One person in the family can own the entire building (he/she may rent out all the units), or different individuals in the family can own each unit.

Many families who own an entire building with multiple units use them as property investing as an ideal investment strategy. It serves as an additional source of income that appreciates steadily in value, improving the overall portfolio. A multifamily real estate business can build a large portfolio for rental units.

That means if you own 20 units in the building, managing is easier and time-efficient. You can also hire a property manager or outsource operations to a property management company to help your family business generate profits.

Now you know the difference between the single-family business and multifamily business, you might be wondering why go for family businesses when lots of businesses are out there? If you're not sure why investing in a family real estate business is a good idea, consider this.

Family businesses can offer:

Stability

Normally, the leadership or headship of a family business is determined by each individual's position in the family. It leads to leadership longevity that ensures better stability in a family-run business. In many real estate family businesses, the leader stays in the position for a long time, and events like retirement, illness, or death, are the main triggers for a position change.

Commitment

You might not have heard this before, but family businesses tend to have a better sense of accountability and commitment at heart compared to non-family businesses.

When you invest funds into a single or multifamily business, it is not only the business needs that you cater to but also family needs. This is when the desire to stay stronger for both the business and family creates additional advantages that include:

- A better understanding of the real estate industry

- Property management

- Effective marketing and sales

Hoshi Ryokan, for instance, is one of the businesses that survived for centuries. Established in 718, the Japanese hospitality business has been in the family for more than 45 generations. This longevity led the owners to a substantial understanding of the history and business, which anyone new to the company will not be able to replicate.

Similarly, the Ford Motor Company had also stayed afloat during tough financial situations when other businesses, such as GM and Chrysler, were desperate to get a bailout. Though there could be many reasons behind Ford's success, the family reputation, financial standing, and name on the line played a vital role in keeping the fighting spirit high.

Flexibility

This is perhaps the best benefit you get from investing in family-run real estate business. It offers people associated with the business a lot of flexibility. Family members can sometimes wear different hats to take on tasks that are outside their official job description. However, nonfamily businesses have delineated responsibilities for each role.

Take the example of Estée Lauder, founder of a cosmetic firm. She was involved in all the aspects of her business. She has never spent a day without promoting her brand as she believed in what she sells. Time Magazine listed her as a business genius in 1998 for setting an example of how flexibility can be incorporated into a business.

Long-term Perspective

Non-family real estate businesses typically develop goals or objectives for the next quarter. Family businesses, on the other hand, think decades ahead. There is no denying that a long-term outlook is always a good way to promote a culture of better decision-making and clear strategy.

Let's show it with an example again. Chief Executive officer of German Otto Group implemented this perspective to achieve great success. After taking over the business from his father in 1949, he began to figure out the possibilities various computer technologies could offer.

In 1995, the brand switched to e-commerce due to this long-term outlook. It became a huge success by 1998 in online sales. The company is still a family affair.

Reduced Cost

Many businesses struggle during challenging times and economic downturns. Mostly, stakeholders or the board of directors has to work out ways that can keep the company afloat while managing salaries and cash flow.

In family-owned businesses, however, the case is different. Family members are often willing to invest in properties or contribute financially to keep the business up and running during hard times. It may involve temporary pay cuts, contributing personal funds, or ceasing the dividends until the company gets back on its feet.

Remember that for family businesses in real estate or any other industry, long-term business success matters the most to survive financially. Ultimately, it offers more flexibility to the business in terms of financial support.

Like these, there are plenty of other benefits of investing in a family business in the real estate industry. But you must be familiar with the most effective ways to establish the property business and generate the profits to reap the rewards.

Don't worry if you have no idea how to go about it, as we have you covered here. The Book includes everything you need to know about investing in a small multifamily real estate business and achieving the financial freedom you have always dreamt of.

CHAPTER 1

SECURE FUTURE

Because of the economic downturn in the country, many people are finding new ways to diversify their investment portfolio. And multi-family real estate business is an ideal investment option to protect against inflation and market fluctuations.

According to Ben Colonomos- founder of PointOne Holdings and owner of a portfolio of multi-family assets worth $730 million, investing in a MFB is a consistent and simple way to secure a future. Ben has spent more than a decade overseeing MFB assets, operating and developing thousands of units, and managing acquisition. He considers this a business the safest way to get long-term returns.

He believes that multi-family apartment units and rentals have the potential to withstand a future downturn. Overall, many experts and professionals see real estate as an excellent investment vehicle. It is because real estate is a hard, tangible asset that can perform well in financial downturns and an inflationary environment.

It has the ability to produce stable cash flow, and that makes the industry an appealing option for family businesses.

People can have the perfect investment vehicle if they combine the increasing value of the property with tax benefits and cash flow. That means if you own a multiunit building or single-family unit, you can become a passive investor without spending substantial time.

Note that some classes of property have more value compared to others. MFB units, particularly, provide a plethora of added benefits for investors.

Wondering what makes a multi-family real estate business more secure than other businesses? Keep on reading to find some substantial reasons.

First, all multi-family operators are active and agile in terms of getting income streams that are based on short-term leases. The operators need to adapt to the changing trends in the marketplace and meet the renters' demands. This ultimately results in improved return on investment or ROI.

Next, the apartment units have remained in demand over the decade. During the last decade, the market has seen a great shift in trends. People are now renting homes. More millennials and baby boomers have shown interest in renting homes over purchasing.

Approximately 37 percent of current homeowners are renters. It is the highest percentage estimated in the last 40 years. The good news is that there is no sign that this trend will change any time soon. Many people prefer spending on experiences instead of purchasing homes. A multiunit building makes renting or modifying a home more flexible.

However, baby boomers are selling their properties to move closer to mainstream, urban cores. They need an upgraded lifestyle and pedestrian-friendly communities. And shifting to a multi-family community is one way to find extraordinary amenities they don't get in homes.

These amenities include everything from resort-style pools, outdoor grilling areas, and top-notch fitness centers to cabanas and stylish clubhouses with creative co-working spaces.

If you have suburban apartments, know that they also attract tons of new buyers and renters due to different reasons. It mainly includes accessibility to important routes, a family-friendly lifestyle, retail options, and proximity to excellent schools. Suburban neighborhoods also provide renters with affordability and flexibility they rarely get in urban cores.

Industrial/office properties, apartments, or units offer an added advantage with a diversified renter base. That means as an investor, you don't need to rely only on large tenants. You have multiple assets to keep you financially secure. Even if you lose one tenant, it will not impact the cash flow or investment return of the multi-family business.

Put simply, a MFB based on a savvy investment strategy is an ideal way to boost income. But you must find the right locations that have the right demographics. Plus, you need to take micro and macroeconomic income trends into account.

As part of your diversified portfolio, multi-family units will appeal to baby boomers and families looking for a dynamic lifestyle. If your assets are close to retail outlets and high-ranking schools, and in proximity to reputable business corridors, and within a metropolitan statistical area, you will surely make a good sum of money every month.

However, if you're investing in a MFB for the first time, you can make the process simple by:

- Identifying a market and subscribing to the mailing lists of major multi-family brokers who serve the market. Investors need to find many deals to choose the best.

- Contacting the brokers in the housing market and getting introductions to the markets team to find the best financing options. You must understand the demands of lenders regarding specific deals and sponsor groups.

- Lining up equity and consulting multiple investors to understand their return expectations to make a real estate deal.

- Researching the top management firms in the submarket, you identify and find their services and charges.

Multi-family investments can result in an average of 8 percent cash-on-cash annually returns and over 18 percent IRR (internal rate of return). While no business is 100 percent recession-proof, a multi-family real estate business is suitable to weather a potential economic downturn.

A Five-Year Step By Step Plan To Grow Your Real Estate Family Business through STACK

So, you're all set to invest in a large multi-family real estate business for its efficiencies, and salability, yet you have doubts that it is unachievable for you. Let's tell you a secret- investing in a multi-family real estate business doesn't have to be overwhelming, nerve-wracking, or intimidating.

In fact, we will tell you a tried and tested method to flatten your learning curve and escalate your progress into more stable and bigger deals. The method is referred to as "the Stack." It is a proven real estate investment strategy that takes your business to the next level with each property purchase by increasing your unit count. Many people use this method to build their real estate portfolio within a few years.

For instance, you can start by purchasing a single-family property. Then, you can move on to a duplex, 4-plex, 6-plex properties, and so on. Once you get into the investment process like this, you will be able to gain a stable position in the commercial multi-family real estate business world and manage higher-level properties. It is because you're pushing, learning, and growing with each purchase.

That is why we mentioned in the beginning that purchasing a single-family home is a relatively safer choice than buying a big commercial multifamily unit right off the bat. And this is "HOW" the Stack makes transitioning to the next level easy and smooth.

Keep in mind that Rome wasn't built in a day, and neither will your business!

Now that you have an idea of how Stack works and what is possible in the domain, we can move forward and explore this path to get into the multi-family real estate business with the stack method.

Double Your Investment Every Year with these Steps

Purchase an SFR/ Live-In Single-Family Home with a Loan Program Using a Low Down Payment

Government-backed loan programs, such as FHA loans, require only a 3.5 percent down payment from borrowers. The borrowers do not need a credit score above 585. They require 10 percent down with scores below this range.

Note that the credit score requirement doesn't remain constant. Often, it fluctuates, depending on the market rates. Plus, if you opt for an FHA loan and put down less than 10 percent, you need to pay for PMI (private mortgage insurance) for the loan duration or until you obtain 20 percent refinance and equity to a conventional loan.

PMI, typically, is a security amount or insurance that you might be required to purchase as a condition of a traditional mortgage loan. It increases your monthly payments and makes it harder to manage cash flow when you shift and rent your unit.

Putting down over 10 percent allows you to request the termination of your private mortgage insurance once you reach 20 percent equity.

Fortunately, the loan type is widely available for borrowers and facilitates them according to their circumstances and preferences. In fact, many US residents use FHA loans to secure their initial investment or buy the first unit. One reason is that most lenders are accustomed to working with this loan type. It makes walking through or navigating the process easier.

There is no denying that if you find a good and reliable mortgage lender to invest in your first property, closing a deal becomes a breeze. This is true no matter what loan type you choose. The USDA and VA loans offer borrowers 100 percent financing. That makes it possible to purchase a property with a $0 down payment.

USDA loans are not much different from FHA loans. They also have private mortgage insurance like FHA loans. However, VA loans don't have any private mortgage insurance. This is why they are considered the best for multi-family business investors.

The expenditures that come with VA loans are the cost of inspection, closing costs, and the appraisal fee. If your deal allows it, the best way to keep costs down is to negotiate the closing costs. It can help you lower the amount of personal investment you need to buy the property. You can purchase a property worth up to $20,500 for just $2,000 out of your pocket.

This quick overview of the government-backed loans was to help you understand how you can execute them in your first step of Stack. However, the only nuance is that you need to use these loans for a primary residence you buy. None of these government entities back your investment loan.

Plus, the loan types require you to live in the investment property for one year.

The plans are subject to changing life circumstances that impact the type of house you need to spend your life comfortably. These may include unplanned children, career changes, or any incident that requires you to change the house.

You should take steps to avoid any kind of mortgage fraud. Inform your lender if you're not planning to live in the property for 12 months, which is often a prerequisite. Many investors get the loan by stating that they will live in the house for a year and then rent it immediately without moving in.

Move to Duplex with a New Homeowner Loan after 1 Year

Once the timeline to live in your primary residence is complete, it is time to take the next step. It is when you actually begin to see some financial growth and feel like a landlord. You have used your property as a test run and are familiar with the buying process.

You know how to work with a real estate agent, analyze properties, work with lenders, and eventually close the property deal with an attorney or title company. You have learned the ins and outs of property purchase and feel comfortable purchasing properties.

Now it is time to close on a duplex. And qualifying for another SFR will help you gain new knowledge and learn several new things to turn your deal into a better investment. You need to rent out the house you have had for one year and a duplex you're investing in. Here you need to polish your property management skills to ensure continued success.

Manage your own properties from the start. It might be necessary at this stage as you may lack the cash, and profits from your rental properties might be low. Even if you have a full-day job, two rental units are very manageable. Learn some tips from Mike Butler's "Landlording on Autopilot" or Brandon Turner's "Managing Rental Properties".

Both are exceptional resources to learn some effective property management tips and rules. They have helped millions of multi-family real estate business owners kickstart their journey. The books have everything you need to learn to successfully screen and select good tenants while managing the property efficiently.

When you manage your units at the beginning, you learn the tricks to deal with tons of things at the same time effectively. When you need to hire a qualified property manager for properties, you will have sufficient experience to supervise them.

Buy a 4-plex (Either a Pure Investment Property or a House Hack)

By the time you reach this stage, you must have been able to put aside some cash flow from your two rental units. You can use the stock-in-trade from your units or a combination of the two with equity gained from the properties. With these funds, you have an opportunity to step up your game and invest in a 4-unit property to grow your investment.

Whether you decide to live in the property or not, you will generate enough revenues to hire a property manager at this point. As you have 6 to 7 rental units now, seeking the assistance of a professional property management company makes sense. It will help you focus on your business and its continued success.

It is worth mentioning that every penny saved in expenses is money you can invest back in your portfolio to expand business or grow faster. So, if you think you can manage units on your own, give it a try.

Step into the Profitable Real Estate World and Invest in an 8-Unit

It has likely been two or three years since you invested in your first unit. Now you have purchased and managed more than five units (ideally). However, with cash flow come repairs and renovations. You have to keep your property updated. At this point, you likely have stable turnover and may have filled vacancies.

You must have had plenty of problems along the route that you needed to learn to solve, such as evictions and clogged toilets. At this stage, you're more experienced and much wiser regarding buying, owning, managing, and financing your multifamily real estate business. Now you have the confidence and poise to up your game to a commercial purchase.

Remember that commercial real estate is different from residential real estate in terms of how it is appraised. It takes various income methods into account rather than just sales comparables in the residential units you've purchased so far.

Before getting in too deep, do your research and focus on cap rates and net operating income (NOI) to estimate the property's value and the amount you can pay for it. And as you have been operating similar units for three years (duplex and 4-plex), you have gained a sound knowledge of the expenses you will need for the 8-plex.

As a smart and savvy investor, you should stick to the same area or location where you have other three properties. It is because you know the area well and don't have to research other rentals in the neighborhood. You have an idea of what the properties will rent out for. Put simply, you're familiar with the expected expenses and income. Now, you can calculate the NOI on your 8-plex unit.

But, it doesn't mean that you shouldn't determine the cap rates of the area. It is important to find out the maximum amount you can or should pay for an 8-plex property to boost your multi-family real estate business. The formula to determine that is **value = net rate/ cap rate**. It allows you to seal the deal when you get the unit that meets your requirements.

When you buy and operate it, you will find out that it is not much different from a 4-plex.

Repeat these Processes and Build or Grow Your Portfolio into Smart Apartment Investing

Remember that each purchase will help you get a deeper understanding of how you can tie things together. The primary principles of a multi-family real estate business, such as purchasing, managing, and financing your SFRs, are no different from apartment complexes. That means you invest right, fund right, and manage right.

The journey involves buying, managing, and financing properties and is full of learning. It develops and polishes your skills while giving you the confidence to continue and close significant deals. Don't forget that the cash flow and equity your venture has built over the years converts into impressive net worth.

Real estate is indeed about being patient, especially for people looking to build wealth. While you can venture into the profitable multi-family business right away, you should have some notable prerequisites to be successful.

If you've just started, it is better to wait. We say this because multi-family real estate investing is one of the proven wealth-building techniques. And when you use "the Stack," improving your success rate becomes much easier. The method or investment strategy continues to push you out of your comfort zone.

What Else!

Know Your Ability in Investing Area

An accurate assessment of a multifamily unit you're interested in investing in is fundamental for long-term success and profitability. If done right, a multi-family real estate business is financially rewarding. But it can backfire if you don't focus on the basics. And one such mistake is overlooking your ability to purchase the right property without any encumbrances.

It is perhaps the first thing you need to evaluate when you find the property.

Here are a few elements you should consider when assessing a multifamily unit.

Due Diligence

It is often difficult to be too careful when assessing a multifamily property. However, you must check the skeletons in the closet before signing a deal. It is because if a property seems impeccable or too good to be true, it may have some risks.

There can be risks in the form of unpaid penalties, violations, and potential pending lawsuits that can turn your revenues into losses. This is especially true if you fail to resolve complicated issues after making a purchase. You need to have the motivation and skills to inspect the investing area carefully.

If you're buying a 4-plex, make sure you inspect the units from top to bottom for potential issues, like structural integrity, leakage, and roofing problems.

Bear in mind that finding every little detail about your prospective property isn't possible regardless of how much you explore. Typically, when you buy a property or become a landlord, you find out various aspects of the investment you make.

Consider Environment, Advantages, and Disadvantages of the Area/Location You Are Investing

Location

Once you identify the rental building to purchase for your multi-family real estate business, it is the right time to evaluate the location. The location and economic conditions of a place play a major role in estimating the value of the asset you'd like to buy. It also impacts the rate of return you will earn from the property.

Be sure you're familiar with the market you want to invest in. If you're a new buyer in a city, study its economic conditions and demographics. Weigh in its negative and positive aspects. Assess if your property has the potential to increase in value in that city. You need to choose a location that guarantees a solid and stable cash flow.

Moreover, the demand and supply of multifamily properties are also pivotal in determining a location. Analyze the location's submarkets. You can divide them by zip code or neighborhood. It will help you get a better and more comprehensive understanding of the housing trends in the city.

Purchasing a multifamily building in an emerging and progressive submarket can ensure a winning investment. However, when you don't have proper knowledge of the location, you may end up buying in an inappropriate neighborhood and lose money.

Do a Comparable Search

It is a straightforward move that you shouldn't miss out on when planning to invest in a multi-family real estate business.

The step entails evaluating nearby buildings (rentals) with the same number of units, types of amenities, and square footage. The comparative research will give you statistics, such as cap rates, NOI, and rent of the property similar to yours.

If the multifamily property you've chosen to invest in has a lower price compared to other assets in the location, you may be lucky to get this deal. When you compare properties in the neighborhood, it helps you find out if you're buying an expensive multifamily property compared to nearby units. Thorough research and analysis can keep you from making a bad decision.

Check the Multifamily Building Yourself or Do Property Tours

If you're serious about purchasing a multifamily property, it is crucial to check the building yourself. You need to examine everything, including common areas, bathrooms, kitchen, roof, and the overall condition. You can visit properties similar to the multifamily property you want to purchase in order to compare the levels of upkeep and several other essential factors.

Following this step increases clarity, and you get a better understanding of the worth of the multifamily building. At this stage, we recommend that you consult professional brokers, tax experts, and lawyers to make an informed decision.

As a property investor, understanding the housing market, evaluating property sales and values isn't enough. You must determine that your investment is a smart move and aligns with your budget and financial goals. Expert investors conduct several property tours to not only spot problems but also identify opportunities.

This is essential for people investing in a multifamily real estate business for the first time. Touring the property allows new investors to network with other buyers or investors. It is a chance to discuss market rents, most sought-after amenities, and operating expenses specific to a submarket. Priceless knowledge!

Put simply, going/looking closely at your chosen multifamily property can offer you these benefits:

The Advantages of Pre-Offer Property Tours

- **Lead to Informed Negotiations.** Allows you to check the condition and state of a property to negotiate a fair market price

- **Determine Cost to Address Delayed Maintenance.** Helps you understand the potential cost of property maintenance tasks that have been delayed by the seller.

- **Determine Capital Upgrade Planning.** Enables you to determine more accurate, reliable, long-term plans to improve home systems, such as alarm systems, fire control systems, and HVAC equipment.

- **Assess Repurposing Opportunities.** Helps you determine if you can incorporate new amenities, improve the property to capture residents' attention.

- **Opportunity to Learn about Tenants.** Helps you figure out if you need to relocate residents. And if you can find tenants that meet the screening criteria in the housing market.

- **Determine the Motivation of the Seller.** As you don't know the seller's intentions, touring the property yourself is one way to determine the seller's motivation.

What Else Can You do?

Speak with Tenants

When visiting a multifamily building, try to speak with tenants. Engage them in a casual conversation when possible. You need to be careful when having this conversation, as most renters don't know that the property or building is for sale. You could politely ask them what amenities they have been provided with. Or what is it they like about this building?

Use this opportunity to speak with on-site managers and other employees. They might give you insight into the things that may impact your purchase.

Check Outside

Scout the neighborhoods by arriving early and getting some exercise within a 5-block walk. The purpose is to know the environment. Once you're at the multifamily building, have a walk around the complex.

Here is what you can look for:

Consider the vehicles- Are the vehicles in the area late models, parked on turf, or in disrepair? If you find a lot of vehicles in the vicinity, it might mean that most tenants in the prospective building are at home.

Look for signs of neglect, poor maintenance, or uncleanliness -

- Are the dustbins overflowing or not discarded?
- Are the common areas or landscape being cleaned and well-maintained?

- Do the benches, patios, or other structures suffer from any damage?
- What is the condition of the foundation and exterior walls?
- Are railings, steps, and sidewalks safe and usable?
- Does the building meet the accessibility requirements and standards?
- Do windows open (if not, there may be problems with the heating and cooling system?)
- Is there clear and maintained signage?

Check the Roof - Roof repair or replacement is an expensive affair; thus, you must check them carefully to see if they need to be redone. Plus, inspect when the last time roof repair was completed? Are scuppers and drains in working order?

Check the Doors - Are the doors opening and closing properly? Do they have any security issue (it can be a sign of any criminal or drug activity)

Look for other Problems- Check if there are any drainage problems or standing puddles in the building. Does the building have any noticeable odor? Does the building have signs of fire damage?

Check Inside

Don't mind spending some more time inspecting. The multifamily building may look good on the outside; however, its interior may require work.

At a minimum, you should ask the seller to show you around each type of residential unit (1, 2 beds, efficiency/studio). Be sure you make notes of each unit before signing the contract.

Inspect the Entrance –

- Is the entrance area welcoming or inviting?
- Is the mail area and lobby clean?
- Does a unit have an entryway security system?
- Are apartment numbers visible?
- Do they have controlled access and security cameras?
- Does this system meet the safety requirements?
- Does the building have a designated area for receiving or accepting deliveries securely?
- Are there egresses, adequate lighting, and exit signage?

Examine the Common Areas - When touring the building's interior, check its facilities and amenities, such as fitness areas and laundry rooms. Visit the boiler room and look for disrepair, date of inspection notices, rust, and safety hazards, including stored materials (inflammable ones). Look for inspection notices on fire extinguishers and elevators.

Look for Damage or Signs of Erosion/Wear and Tear - Once inside the unit, look for ceiling stains, cracks, and other damage. Check if floors and windows are old or warped. Do windows and doors fit well? Is there a need to update property aesthetics, like flooring, hardware, counters, fixtures, and flooring?

Check Storage Areas - Don't forget to inspect the storage units carefully.

Look for Tenant Notices, Management Signs, and Bulletin Boards - Even a short statement or warning on tenant notices can reveal a lot.

Look out for Other Problems - Are there traps or pests? Does the unit have noises or sounds?

How to Make Your Investment Profitable

Focusing on the little details mentioned above can play a crucial role in increasing the value of multifamily property. The main purpose is to invest in a multi-family real estate business that allows you to generate higher profits by adding amenities to the complex.

If the units need upgrades, you can estimate the cost of repairs and how it can contribute to the rents you will charge from your tenants. It is important to set the rent after considering housing market trends.

If the standard rent of the property is higher, the net operating investment will also be higher. It will automatically increase the cash flow and value of the property. You maintain the occupancy of your investment property at a higher rate to maximize the profits.

If your multifamily property has additional, unused space, you need to find ways to use the space wisely to increase your income. If your budget permits, you have an option to demolish the building and rebuild something (on demand) from scratch. You have the option to build a couple of floors on the current structure if it is legally permissible.

Find Your Comfort Zone Where You Can Invest

Did you know your comfort zone is proportional to your beliefs?

Is there anything you can do to expand your comfort zone proactively in the multifamily real estate business?

Yes, there are ways you can practically find and improve your comfort zone when investing in multifamily buildings.

Start by Visualizing

It is an important step you shouldn't miss out on. You need to visualize yourself touring the units or buildings you want to buy, negotiating with sellers, and making a contract. Just like professional athletes visualize themselves beating the records, performing at a high level, and receiving a medal, you need to strengthen your imagination.

Imagining yourself in the desired multiunit building will help you figure out what you would like to see in your investment asset and what is your comfort zone. See yourself finalizing the deal of a building in 5 years and receiving a $450,000 payment at closing.

Make a Simple Deal

The next step ensures that you know what you want to do; therefore, try to make it a simple deal.

Wondering what a simple deal is?

A simple deal means a document describing your multifamily property. Everything in your deal is REAL:

description, financials, business plans, projected returns, and photos. The only thing that makes it different from a real deal is that you have not signed a contract yet.

You can use this deal package as a tool to act as if you own an apartment building. Don't forget to review your financials and the marketing package here. Assume that you have made projections and assumptions. Acting "as-if" makes you feel like it is real and increases your passion for turning your dream business into a reality.

It doesn't end here as you can use your deal package to discuss things with potential investors, which is often the most challenging part. Tell them that you may sign a contract in the future and show them the multifamily building as a representative or the kind of deal you're looking for.

The step may seem insignificant, but it can help you find and expand your comfort zone. In fact, use it to develop credibility with your sellers, investors, and other experts on your team.

Visit Multifamily Buildings

Another simple way to find and get out of your comfort zone is to visit buildings that you really want to invest in. For instance, if your current comfort zone is a multifamily building between 70 and 90 units, see yourself finding and finalizing the deal, collecting the money, renovating it, and generating profits from it.

However, you can expand your comfort zone by visiting a 150 unit multifamily building- that seems impossible to buy or overwhelming because of the amount. By visiting these units, you can analyze them and think of ways to work on a deal that needs substantial capital investment and management.

It is undeniably a long shot, but going through this process can help you think big and get out of your comfort zone. Keep in mind that pushing yourself to see, experience, and think out of your comfort zone is a great exercise to visualize the things you CAN do. It strengthens your belief and forces you to think of ways to make your multi-family real business dream a reality.

Need an extra tip?

Find out your multifamily building's insurance requirements.

New constructions have several unique features when it comes to insurance. And the same is true for your multifamily real estate building. If you neglect these features, it may expose your business to potential losses, including the risks of theft, fire, and property damage.

So how much insurance coverage do you need for your apartment building?

When insuring a multifamily building that is new construction, your expected cost of construction must be equal to the total dwelling coverage amount. It is one way to ensure that if you lose the "total sum" of your construction being built, you will receive an amount close to the sum you invested in the property. Your settlement amount is settled on the capital you invested at the time of damage or loss with the construction of a new building.

Do You Need Liability Insurance for a Multifamily Property?

To answer this question, yes, you need liability insurance for a new multifamily property. It is because new properties may face direct property damage. In fact, liability coverage is essential for investing in newly constructed properties.

There is no right or wrong coverage amount to carry. Properties that are under construction or being built from the ground up have higher liability exposure. Typically, they need higher limits of more than $1MM per occurrence that makes an aggregate of $2MM.

As mentioned above, even one fall may cost property owners thousands of dollars. We recommend you invest in an umbrella policy according to the investment portfolio size and risks associated with your multifamily property. Also, there are several risks you may face when you use your homeowner's liability insurance policy for new construction. So, you need to keep business line liability separate from personal ones.

What Deductible should you Carry for a New Multifamily Project?

Bear in mind that deductibles are the portion of the money you pay out of your pocket for any losses at your property before an insurer pays for a claim.

Consider the lowest claim you need to file and increase it twice when estimating a deductible. You get a higher rate if you lower the property deductible. Choosing a higher deductible means that you will be able to generate savings that are enough to make up for the difference.

Cost of New Construction Insurance

The insurance cost of new multifamily construction may vary depending on many factors. Some of them include:

- The desired insured amount
- Deductibles
- Level of coverage

Know that insurance for new multifamily construction may cost you thousands of dollars as they are at high risk of damage.

However, it doesn't mean that the cheapest insurance coverage is the best coverage. This is particularly true for new constructions. You must speak with an expert insurance agent to determine the items your property covers.

CHAPTER 2

SINGLE FAMILY VS. MULTIFAMILY INVESTING

Whether you agree or not, the debate "single-family vs. multifamily investing" exists. In fact, the debate confuses and attracts property investors when it comes to making a decision. Each option promises better benefits than the other does, and for good reasons.

If you're an experienced property investor, you must be aware of the fact that both single-family and multifamily investments have a separate place in the housing market. And choosing between single-family and multifamily property largely depends on your personal preferences and financial goals.

The landscape of real estate investing is not only varied but also largely opportunistic. This is the primary reason many investors claim why they got into the industry in the first place. The industry is full of lucrative opportunities for people ready to put in the legwork. They can find opportunities in different shapes and sizes to invest and make profits, especially in the long run.

While some investors make a comfortable living by buying and selling properties, others are content with generating passive income by purchasing and holding assets. It is because there can be many ways to earn profits in real estate. In fact, if you're a smart investor, you can use different exit strategies to make a reasonable profit in the current market environment.

It is worth mentioning that the differences between single-family and multifamily investment don't just end here. You can break each real estate exit strategy into additional categories: wholesaling, rental properties, and rehabbing. Interestingly, each category offers savvy entrepreneurs and investors an opportunity to invest in or finance either multifamily or single-family property.

That said, if you're up for the challenges, you could find many options. However, if you lack sufficient literacy and experience in investing in single-family and multifamily properties, you may feel overwhelmed. It is especially true if you're not experienced and skilled at multi-family real estate investment strategies.

Luckily, the single vs. multifamily investing debate is more interesting than intimidating. And if you're among the one who wants to learn, keep scrolling down. Let's know the fundamental differences between the two major investment types, including their benefits and downsides.

Multifamily Investing Benefits

To reiterate, a multifamily residential property has multiple units. That means it has two or more separate sets of owners. Note that if the building has more than five units, it includes commercial, residential property. It impacts the financing and loans you would obtain.

At its core, multi-family real estate business or investing considers macroeconomic conditions. This means that if you have an insufficient supply with high demand, the price of an asset tends to increase. Here are the major things that differentiate a multi-family real estate business from a single-family home.

Higher Cash Flow

You might have heard that cash is king. This is probably why folks who get to choose between a lottery and a lifetime annuity pick the former. However, at the end of the day, it is the cash flow that really matters.

It is worth noting that cash is not only king but also more crucial than just having money. You may find many people in the market who liquidate their investments and let the cash sit idle. But they never solve the issue of needing to generate a consistent cash flow.

Put simply, with a consistent cash flow, you can remove the need to sell assets at the wrong time, especially when values go down. Plus, when you generate a sufficient cash flow, you don't have to worry about economic downturns.

However, having a portfolio that stresses income-generating assets is pivotal to generating consistent cash flow. It can be anything from interest-paying bonds, private equity investing, dividend-producing stocks, and real estate investing.

But not all investments you make for cash flow are equal-you must have a reliable asset such as a multi-family investment. It is one of the consistent cash flow investments. In fact, the biggest advantage you get from investing in multi-family real estate business is the promise of generating monthly cash flow from your rental.

How it generates cash flow

Single-family properties can have only one renter or group of tenants; multifamily apartment buildings have multiple renters. Even if one unit has a vacancy, you will likely have monthly cash flow coming from other units.

If you've the right investment strategy in place, are getting the fair market price for units, and generating rental income that doesn't exceed your NOI (property management, mortgage payment, taxes, property maintenance, and insurance), you're all set to obtain a bigger cash flow.

It also shows that your apartment building is in a strong market, and you will be able to fill the vacant units quickly. Make your multi-family investment decisions based on "not risking principle" to get bigger cash flow.

When you have a sizeable portion of investment in an income-generating asset, it gives you more freedom and flexibility with the other assets in your portfolio. That means if you invest in a multifamily property within one region, things such as a natural disaster can put your asset at risk.

But if you purchase a multi-family real estate building across geographically diverse areas, with a diverse employer base and tenant base, it brings consistency in the cash flow.

Making this type of multifamily real estate investment generates a cash flow that can hedge against any equity risk. The right multifamily investment can be a great alternative.

For example, multi-family property investment in an attractive location across markets can offer you protection during an economic downturn.

So how can you leverage your multi-family real estate investments for bigger cash flow?

Though we have mentioned some tips above, here are some more.

You can invest in multifamily properties or apartment buildings and manage the assets yourself. But the strategy requires too much effort and may lack diversification.

Consider taking multi-family investment financing to get through the economic cycle. Choosing and obtaining the best funds can provide you with a consistent cash flow throughout the market cycle. Consult with a multifamily real estate business expert to find the best cash flow-oriented, multifaceted strategy that can deliver consistent, steady high returns even when the market is down.

Moreover, you can:

- Invest in affordable workforce houses as these multi-family investments can produce a 10 percent cash-on-cash return. Thousands of tenants pay this income every month.
- Buy value-added properties or assets that generate cash flow while focusing on improving that income through strategies, such as renovations and updates.
- Diversify the properties, including thousands of apartment buildings across the US. If you want to expand this idea, consider investing in high-end real estate that may have advantages that are hard to find domestically. For instance, if you buy a property in the Atlantic Ocean

in British territory, you don't have to pay capital gains and yearly property taxes when transferring the property.

That means multifamily real estate abroad offers protected ownership under a land registry. The islands use US dollars as the official currency, which means exchange rates will not affect the purchasing process or future value of your property.

Though the global pandemic has impacted the buying and selling process to some extent, the islands still make a good investment option. We say this because the cost of land has significantly increased over the decade.

Thanks to growing development and a thriving tourism culture, the prices are likely to increase more in the future, as per Blair Macpherson – broker and co-owner of Real Estate Groups. Property investors can make an additional income by renting these properties even while away. They can hire a property manager to handle the process.

However, it is worth mentioning that investing in an international property may have some unique challenges. Different countries have different ways to regulate real estate issues, especially when investing in a multifamily apartment building.

That is why you need to make this decision once you have sufficient knowledge of how real estate works in the country you're considering. Of course, you don't want to invest in a property abroad that can be easily taken back by the foreign government down the road.

Buy a luxury condo to rent out. Investing in a property located in a luxury building with necessary transportation and amenity options nearby is a wise idea to earn steady cash flow.

Know that a good location can make a huge difference when it comes to investing in multifamily real estate. Purchasing a property in a luxurious building with no or poor transportation options might not benefit you as much as you expect.

In addition to location and transportation, other features and services the building offers to residents also make or break the investment. By other features, we don't mean that your high-end property should have a full-time watchman.

However, it means "what else your property offers," and that may include terraces, high ceilings, and views. You might think these features are not significant, but these can be the defining feature of your home. They play an important role in distinguishing your home from other conventional and ready-made apartment buildings that lead to high selling rates.

You must remember that buying multifamily real estate equates to purchasing a lifestyle. Features like swimming pools, private roofs, fitness centers, decks, common spaces, and maid services set luxury real estate apart from cookie-cutter apartments. Even if there is a new condo built around the home you purchase, it will still hold value.

More Control over Value

Multifamily investments or real estate businesses continue to be one of the reliable sources to give you above-average returns. According to a recent study, multifamily apartment buildings add to a healthy economy with more lifetime tenants, interest rates, and shifts in housing markets.

Many investors refer to the profits or revenues from real estate as "mailbox money." It instantly shows up in the mailbox from your smart investments. Note that investing in a multi-family real estate business creates a unique snowball effect for investors. They can leverage it to grow their real estate portfolio using various financing options.

Once they acquire more properties, it increases their net worth. This is when they have enough capital to qualify for or finance more multifamily properties. They can upgrade these properties to improve the value of their apartment buildings.

In fact, you can leverage it as a gateway that can allow you to control multifamily real estate. We say this because the values of multifamily real estate depend on NOI (profitability of real estate investments) and cap rates. A slight change in NOI can significantly increase the value of the properties.

Thus, when you know how to control your multi-family real estate and how to manage the assets to improve NOI, you have control over value as well as net worth. Multi-family real estate can put you into a controlling position. Though you cannot control the regulations and rules that govern the housing market, you can pick and choose your future easily and actively.

Take a look at these points if you are wondering how real estate puts you in a controlling position.

- You have a choice to pick and select a strong market, such as buying luxury homes that have high value regardless of market condition
- You can add more value by making unique renovations, improvements and adding exclusive features to the apartment building
- You can rent multiple properties, such as vacation rentals, to create long-term passive income
- You can buy or sell instantly when the real estate market is up

No other investment or saving plan offers investors this level of flexibility and control.

So, how can you do it?

Complete a Custom-Built Multifamily Property

If things go right, a custom-built multifamily property offers the highest profits margins. Though it may have a longer time frame, if you know how to make money from this option, it is beneficial. A multifamily building designed with desired styles and advanced features can get you a high income.

If you intend to build the multifamily building for investment, make sure you customize it in a way that appeals to a broad segment of the high-end real estate market. A custom-built building with state-of-the-art amenities, finishes, and layouts maximizes its chances of selling for top dollars.

Plus, you need to ensure that the property you're renting is functional, has required privacy and security with a welcoming feel for buyers. However, there is a subtle line between building an appeal for the buyers and creating exclusivity that homeowners or tenants crave.

When you don't commoditize the multifamily property but make it desirable, this is when the demand and price really jump. Take the example of '82 Lafitte Rothschild's bottle appreciated in price over a less superior vintage due to supply and demand. The same applies to a multifamily real estate business. The harder it is to find, the more valuable the property becomes.

Larger Pool of Tenants

Multifamily real estate has gained a significant amount of comparative edge in terms of rising tenant demand. People look for long-term property investment, regardless of the state's economy. And that has shifted the momentum towards multifamily properties.

Moreover, downsizing millennials and baby boomers are no more interested in buying or owning homes. Many millennials are abandoning their home-buying plans and opting for rentals first, such as multifamily units.

Though renters are always on the move, creating vacancies, you will rarely find a multi-family property that's completely vacant. It means that despite having vacancies, the multifamily owner still has consistent cash flowing in.

A recent survey from Statista found that the average rate of vacancy in multi-family apartment buildings in the US is between 5.7 percent and 6.4 percent. A vacancy in a single-family home, however, means no rents and no cash flow until the new tenants shift in. This makes multi-family real estate investing ideal for a steady cash flow stream.

Allowing more tenants to live in a multi-family building helps owners offset losses they may face due to vacancies.

Scalability

If you want to expand or improve your investment portfolio, there is perhaps no better way than investing in a multi-family real estate business. It offers you multiple opportunities to jump to commercial real estate investment as larger multifamily units and get greater cash flow.

For instance, if you purchase a residential building with 25 units, it makes a cheaper and less time-consuming option compared to acquiring 25 separate single-family properties.

Plus, you will have to deal or negotiate with different sellers, apply for 20 loan types, and conduct individual inspections.

Generating a steady passive income is a part of the multifamily real estate equation and allows you to create a sizeable landed property portfolio. And that makes it more scalable. If you choose a short-term rental strategy, you can set a dynamic price strategy for your apartment building, regardless of the season.

Moreover, if you opt for traditional real estate, it offers you an opportunity to capitalize on ideal locations to get high financial rewards. Unlike other saving options, multifamily real estate helps you diversify your portfolio and enjoy appreciation on each investment.

It is you who has all the authority to make a decision. You can grow your real estate business as much as you want.

Though sometimes buying an apartment building or a multifamily property is a costlier option, banks or financial institutes are more likely to grant mortgage approval for it. It is because the type of property generates consistent cash flow. So even if you have vacancies in your apartment building, they will not cause loss.

In addition to that, multifamily real estate investing is significantly less time-consuming than purchasing single-family homes. That means even one transaction can produce a quicker increase than having separate transactions. If you prefer building an extensive investment portfolio for steady rental income, seeking the help of real estate brokers is the best way to navigate the process and achieve your goals faster.

Also, remember that multifamily property holds value even if it doesn't generate immediate cash. The value increases over time. But it is essential to maintain the multifamily property if you want its value to increase to get a good boost. It is one way to receive a good rental price, attract potential renters, make more cash flow, and build an excellent portfolio.

How about putting in a pool and adding its value to each unit in your multifamily property?

If you have big goals, investing in a multi-family real estate business helps make big leaps!

Ideal for Property Management

Management of a multifamily apartment building is considered more daunting and challenging than single-family property management. In reality, the scenario is different when you hire an experienced and trained property manager.

Remember that qualified property managers prefer to invest their time and effort in handling multifamily units, in contrast to single-family ones. It allows the managers to focus the efforts on just one location instead of traveling to multiple separate houses.

Wondering if paying for property management is worth it for your multifamily building?

No matter how long you have been in the multifamily real estate business, maintaining a healthy and stable stream of revenues can be challenging. That means whether you purchase a residential or commercial apartment building, some headaches and hassles are inevitable.

It requires loads of hard work as well as patience on the part of a property owner to find potential tenants and maintain the property in its prime condition. A reputable property management firm can offer great help when it comes to simplifying the duties of a landlord.

The company specializes in the real estate business and provides quality services to property owners and tenants. It can also optimize cash flow while handling legal issues and disputes. A property management firm saves you from dealing with renters daily. Its responsibilities include more than just collecting and managing payments from tenants.

When you hire a property management firm for your multifamily real estate business, it helps you advertise units, interview, and screen potential tenants, handle move-ins and outs, deal with complaints, draw up the lease, and handle late payments simultaneously.

Since the firm is familiar with all the legal aspects of the owner/renter relationship, it can handle each party with ease. These firms have a professional understanding of handling all the necessary paperwork. They can find, screen, or check the credit card reports of prospective tenants for your multifamily units. The firms conduct background checks, draw up lease agreements, handle the bills, and account for monthly or annual rent for you. In short, the firm will maintain all the required paperwork and you will not have to worry about the technicalities and legal aspects of the real estate business.

Moreover, if you have been in a situation where the water heater in one of your units stopped working or the roof of another unit started leaking at the same time, then you must be familiar with the hassle and stress the situation causes.

So, no matter how experienced or responsible you are as a landlord when it comes to handling multiple units simultaneously, it is not an easy job. Hiring a property management firm is the best solution for problems like these.

Competent property managers efficiently handle everything, whether fixing an old roof or a damaged staircase. To some extent, being an owner of multifamily units requires utmost efficiency and diligence. Paying to a property management firm can make handling your multifamily real estate business a breeze.

The multifamily real estate industry has seen a huge shift in investment, particularly in rental and commercial investments. Property management companies take care of your multifamily property to keep the rising market completion ahead. Property managers are now more vigilant and invest their time tracking more portfolios.

A multifamily building requires skillful and competent employees, along with the right processes to improve and expand the business. If you don't incorporate effective processes to manage your multifamily business, the revenues may suffer.

Many property managers use tricks to maintain or manage a multifamily real estate business. Typically, they do the following.

Use Property Management Software

Effective organization is the key to running the operations of any business. When it comes to managing a multifamily real estate business, there are plenty of details you need to maintain. You need to manage the information relating to units, tenants, contractors as well as properties.

Using cloud-based software to maintain the details will help multifamily property managers access the details anytime, even when they are on the go. Plus, it provides you and the managers with essential information when you are on-site or visiting the properties.

Leverage Digital Platforms

Living in the digital world, you cannot deny the significance of digital platforms. That means moving your tenant communication, and payment systems online is a great way to connect with current multifamily tenants and prospects.

It saves time for not only you but your clients also. That is why property managers leverage digital platforms to improve the operations of a multifamily real estate business.

Use Automation

One trick that property managers use to improve the productivity of your multifamily real estate business is using automation. From paying monthly bills, submitting forms, and reminding tenants about their due payments to using advanced software, they perform tasks automatically. These automatic reminders, payments, and emails will help you reduce your workload.

Ensure Tasks Organization

One important way to grow a successful multifamily real estate business is to finish the tasks at the right time. Whether checking credit or going through references, doing tasks at the right time will save you from the hassle of sending notices or warnings.

Create Content to get Found

Your multifamily real estate business depends on potential tenants. Creating content like relevant blogs and articles with adequate knowledge will help you grab the attention of prospective renters. Property managers update them on a website to maintain the online presence of your multifamily real estate business.

Running a multifamily real estate business is not easy. If you hire a reputed property management company or an experienced manager, they can make the job easier. Most of them use online platforms and advanced software to boost your multifamily real estate business and save time. It increases the productivity of your multifamily real estate business.

Tax Benefits

This might sound strange to you, but investing in a multifamily real estate business can offer some fantastic tax benefits. That means you subtract the cost of maintenance and operations, such as property management, utilities, repair, and maintenance fees. It may also include marketing costs and insurance premiums.

Moreover, many multifamily property owners take advantage of tax benefits generated by real estate depreciation. It is valid even if the market value of the building is increasing.

Remember that an apartment building is a physical structure that comprises a complex network of various systems, such as air conditioning, plumbing, roofing, and electrical systems. The systems have a long useful lifespan and are costly. Over time, the physical state of these systems starts deteriorating with exposure to different elements.

This is where the role of depreciation comes into play. It is an accounting concept allowing owners of a multifamily apartment building to expense one portion of the structure's value to account for deterioration each year. The expense is reflected in the income statement and helps you reduce the net operating income of your property, resulting in reduced tax liability.

Blanket Insurance Policies

Blanket insurance refers to a set of protections that you don't get in an individual policy. While it is costlier, the covered risks make it a worthy investment. In the multifamily real estate business, blanket insurance has become fairly common.

Many real estate investors opt for this type of homeowner's insurance to cover the structure and content of the building units against loss. It is because blanket insurance provides a single limit that landlords can use for their multifamily apartment units.

Using blanket insurance for a multifamily real estate business can:

- Cover multiple units in a single setting or the same property type in multiple locations and in different situations.
- Cover personal belongings in a house.
- Enable consumers to buy and customize blanket insurance.
- Cover multiple rental, commercial, or residential properties.

If you have multiple properties or have complex health insurance needs, you may find blanket insurance less expensive. You may also add riders to your blanket insurance policies. In general, a blanket insurance policy for multifamily property includes:

- Blanket programs

- Policies for first loss
- Policies for first loss limit
- Master policies
- Layered programs
- Property programs
- Master programs
- Pooled programs
- Pooled insurance
- Shared limit policies
- Programs that insure multiple locations in the same policy

Blanket policies for multifamily real estate businesses are acceptable if:

- All requirements and conditions are met
- The terms endorsement doesn't lower, exclude, or limit required coverage.

If you don't own a multifamily building or don't have complex health insurance needs, the blanket policy might not be suitable for you. It is only cost-effective for people with more than two properties. Whether you have multiple rentals, commercial units, or residential properties, blanket insurance is ideal.

But you must evaluate your blanket insurance policies as the terms may vary case by case. We recommend you to work with an experienced insurance agent who knows customizable coverages that can fit your unique needs and preferences.

A blanket policy for multifamily real estate costs about 10 percent more than typical insurance policies. But when you bundle insurance into your blanket policy, it saves you a lot of money that you might not be able to do with a conventional homeowner's insurance policy.

In addition to that, your multifamily apartment building can particularly benefit from blanket mortgage insurance. Typically it's a single mortgage that offers coverage for more than one real estate unit. For instance, if you want to sell the property, hold it as collateral for a mortgage.

However, selling individual units without releasing the mortgage is more beneficial. A blanket mortgage makes getting finance easy for your multifamily properties. There is no need to obtain different mortgages if you're availing this option.

Who can Benefit from Blanket Mortgages?

It is particularly beneficial for real estate investors, flippers, and developers. You can take out the blanket mortgage or blanket loans as an investor for your apartment building to cover buying and renovating expenses of units. You can divide the mortgage amount into many lots.

Most investors acquire multifamily units within a huge purchase and sell them in many individual parts. If you're a house flipper, you can seek this mortgage to leverage the opportunities available in the housing market. Opting for this mortgage option can get you more flexibility to avail various options.

Single Family Investing Benefits

Single-family investing is a better option if you have low investment capital. You can start a property investment business with little or even no money. However, you must find the right investment option to benefit from passive income.

As a new single-family investor, you can only make profits from your single-family property if you do research. You need to study and assess the real estate landscape before investing. If you don't evaluate your buying power, it will be hard to draft a profitable investment strategy.

A single-family real estate can be your go-to plan if you have a growth-type investment strategy to benefit your saving rate in the long run.

For instance, if you decide to invest in a real estate investment trust, it may benefit you. The opportunity holds a portfolio of marketable real estate.

But owning a commercial property using REITs is way more valuable than having a single investment property. It is because you invest in different properties in various locations. It can give you better diversification than a single property.

Another significant benefit you get when you invest in a REIT is starting with a couple of thousand dollars. Plus, there is no need to manage your REIT like an investment property. Purchasing an investment property, in contrast, requires you to pay a larger capital for the down payment.

Did you know REITs can also outperform stocks?

Even if they don't, they still make a valuable asset for young investors.

Let's delve into the details to find some benefits of investing in single-family property.

More Affordable

Usually, single-family properties are less expensive than multifamily buildings. That means if you have a limited investment budget, it is a better option for you.

You will need a relatively lower down payment compared to a multifamily building. In some cases, single-family property owners have to spend less on insurance and maintenance. And that is what makes it a cheaper option.

Higher Appreciation

Single-family property tends to appreciate more compared to multifamily units or condos. However, it usually depends on the location and several other factors. The ROI may vary, and cash flow can also fluctuate.

The larger investment return on the resale is the reason why many investors consider getting into the game a wise decision. A single-family unit usually has a larger return on investment at resale.

Easier to Finance

Some people can afford the upfront cost of multi-family, but most investors are looking to make a smaller investment with lower risk — and that means considering single-family properties.

The numbers are generally bigger when you deal with a multifamily building. It includes multiple units that generate streams of stable revenue. But financing a multifamily complex requires a larger investment upfront to produce that revenue.

Put simply, if you can't pay for your single-family property, you will need financing. And managing funds with a single-family is far easier. In most cases, financing a single-family unit is less expensive than multi-family funding. Typically, you can finance a single-family unit with fixed rates loans, and high loan-to-value ratios.

Easier to Manage

When an investor invests in a larger multifamily building, such as an apartment complex or building, it may involve many management responsibilities (unless they hire a property manager). The duties also add up and make managing units more expensive. However, a single-family home requires investors to upkeep only one yard, a few toilets, and an HVAC system.

The scenario is a little different when it comes to managing a multi-family building.

The investor has to maintain these systems for multiple units many times during the year. For instance, if you're an owner of an apartment complex, you need backup generators installed in the building in case there is a power breakdown.

It requires a different set of skills to maintain and keep the systems running. The larger items cause bigger problems, and if you're making this investment for the first time, all these issues can be a huge headache to deal with on your own.

Single-family homes, in contrast, have fewer household items naturally. They are easier to maintain or manage and typically require fewer capital expenditures that come with investment property. In fact, if you have recently renovated a property, or bought a new home, you might not have to spend on repair and maintenance when renting out.

In some cases, first-time investors can manage the property themselves to gain experience and save money. Handling or managing a multi-unit yourself is a full-time job. Single property management, however, is often easier and hassle-free.

CHAPTER 3

ENTERING INTO MULTIFAMILY INVESTMENTS

When it comes to multifamily investing, it is excellent to be a property owner. Apartment vacancies, as well as interest rates, have remained significantly low during the past few years. Plus, they are likely to stay low for the next few months. That means investing in real is a smart way to not only earn income but also diversify your portfolio.

When planned strategically, the investment generates a steady and consistent return. It wouldn't be wrong to say that real estate investment is an excellent idea to create and build wealth. Investing in properties offers you long-standing financial security. If your cash flow is steady, real estate investing is like a reward that brings many financial benefits for a long time.

For example, if you own a rental property, it offers you a sense of security as the property's value appreciates over time. That means your property's value will increase as both buildings and land are appreciating assets.

Another <u>benefit of investing in real estate</u> that makes it an ideal investment is that it acts as a hedge against inflation. If the inflation rate is high, the property value and rental income increase significantly. That is why all real estate investors make a lot of money during inflation because their cash flow goes up.

Plus, you'd be surprised to know that the rental income you receive monthly from your single-family unit or multifamily building is enough to pay your expenses that also include your mortgage payments. You can make your tenants pay the mortgage just by keeping them happy and mitigating the negative consequences of vacancy at any cost.

Further, as an investor, you can protect your property income from taxes by claiming depreciation. Real estate investors can access a growing pool of debt capital.

It explains why more than 60 percent of the commercial lending, which is expected to reach $800 billion in 2022, goes to multifamily real estate investment projects.

Remember that saving money in banks can never benefit you financially in the long run. It does not maximize your wealth. In fact, high inflation, interest, and tax reduce the value of hard-earned money. That is why you must have a reliable investment option, such as real estate, which offers you tons of investing benefits, such as steady income, long-term financial security, and tax benefits.

You may find plenty of professionals other than mortgage bankers who look forward to doubling their profits through investing in multifamily housing. A recent survey from the National Real Estate Investor's survey ranked multifamily real estate business the most <u>attractive commercial investment</u>. The primary reasons are appreciation, rental income, and tax advantages.

Need more convincing? Here is a breakdown of the reasons that make the multifamily real estate business the best investment.

Reasons to Invest in Multifamily Real Estate

Multifamily Property Can Multiply Your Income with Only Incremental Added Cost

In most housing markets, anyone can finance a small multifamily property the same way they purchase a house with an FHA, VA, or conventional loan. They may have to pay slightly higher interest rates or need to have a larger capital reserve depending on their lender. A multi-family property tends to increase your income with incremental added cost.

That is why investing in multifamily rental has become one of the most preferred investment strategies for many investors who need additional monthly income. It benefits the owner with slow but steady and consistent value appreciation. As multifamily properties are apartment complexes or buildings, they have more rental space.

With fewer barriers to market entry, investing in apartment complexes has plenty of benefits. All you need is a high-risk strategy for flipping and fixing to increase your building's value. It typically happens because many markets have primary buyers who are investors, not owner-occupants.

Multifamily houses are valued based on their generated NOI (net operating income). It means any value-added work done on your property leads to a bigger NOI and higher rents. It will also increase the market value of a multifamily home.

Multifamily Rentals are Simpler to Finance, Return Profit Quickly, and Benefit from Economies of Scale

The cost of buying an apartment complex is higher than buying a single-family house in most cases. A single-unit rental property may cost a buyer as little as $20, 000 to $30,000, whereas the cost of an apartment complex may go up to millions.

At a glance, it may seem that securing funds or a loan for a single-family property is a lot easier than collecting finances for a million-dollar complex. But the truth is different. In reality, banks and various lenders tend to approve more loans for multifamily than an average home.

The reason is straightforward. A multi-family real estate business generates a steady and better cash flow. This also applies if your multifamily building has a few vacancies with some tenants making late payments. However, if a renter leaves a single-family home, it becomes 100 percent vacant.

A ten or 15 unit property with one vacancy means only 10 percent of the property would be unoccupied. It reduces the risk of a foreclosure on a multifamily building, in contrast to a family rental. This equates to a relatively less risky investment for banks and lending institutions. It also results in more or better competitive interest rates for buyers, investors, and property owners.

It doesn't end here as multi-family real estate is a better and faster-growing market when it comes to compounding returns. When you invest in larger cities or states with a low affordability ratio, you don't have much room for appreciation.

Also, returns don't reflect the risks investors are usually exposed to. The approach is very visible in the market outlook of the National Association of Realtors. The market predicts <u>favorable conditions</u> in regions where apartment rents are more affordable with low vacancies.

Keep in mind that as a multi-family real estate business owner:

- Your goal is to make more profits per property, collect more profitable units, and create a vibrant portfolio.
- Brokers are responsible for 90 percent of closings. So, make sure you network with excellent brokers in the markets to close good deals.
- The investors who build the most vibrant real estate portfolio are the ones who analyze or evaluate multiple deals every week. It is all about how you maintain the deal flow.
- Don't lose the property if it has high potential but has minor repairs or issues.

In addition to these key benefits, the multi-family real estate business is raging in popularity due to its superior advantages of operating at scale. It doesn't mean that one requires a bigger cash investment to earn profits. It means leveraging large properties that have multiple units or more assets. And you can do it easily through syndication and partnerships.

Remember that the best real estate investment is one that enjoys the most financial growth, earns a profit, and benefits from <u>economies of scale</u> (EOS). The benefit is the economic advantage you gain as the business operates on a larger scale.

EOS can impact various areas of this investment, including expenses appreciation, safety/risk, and principal pay-down, and tax savings. In fact, it is a great way to decrease risk and keep your money safe. No matter how experienced you're in real estate, life happens, and some things are unavoidable.

Your tenants may have to relocate, experience the loss of a loved one, job loss, and go through an array of reasons that can cause them financial instability. With benefits like EOS that you get by investing in a multifamily property, you don't have to worry about bad luck striking you any moment.

It is because a complex with 30 to 50 units with 75 percent break-even occupancy will have more than half of the vacancies before it becomes a risky investment.

Growing a Portfolio Takes Less Time

A multi-family real estate business makes an ideal option for property investors who want to develop a larger portfolio of units. Plus, acquiring an apartment complex with 20 units is less time-consuming and easier than buying 20 different single homes.

Investing in a single-family home will need you to work with 20 different home sellers back and forth. Don't forget the inspections of the properties that you will do by visiting each location individually. In some cases, the route requires investors to qualify for 20 separate loans for the properties. But you can avoid this headache by buying just one property with 20 units.

It shows that when you invest in a multi-family property, it is a cost-effective way to scale the property portfolio without financing a single property at a time.

Costly but Easier To Finance

Residential multi-family property has the lowest entry barriers and is simplest to finance. That is why most multifamily investors get started. You may find many investors who own and occupy only one unit in the first rental building to secure attractive financing.

If you team up with the right lender to get through the entire financing process, you can create a consistent and strong cash flow. However, be sure that you have a sufficient understanding of your financing options to choose the best for your needs. You can select the most suitable one from the given options for your financing needs:

- FHA loans
- Bridge loans
- CMBS Loans
- Agency Loans
- Bank loans

Strong Rental Demand from Millennials

This might seem surprising to you, but more than <u>38 percent of millennials</u> (born between 1981 and 1996) represent the largest share of buyers in the US, according to the National Association of Realtors.

In fact, the wealthy millennials are going big by breaking the concept of "starter homes" that generation X embraced. While baby boomers retire to sunnier locales, remote work has enabled millennials to climb the housing ladder in more affordable and smaller cities, as stated by Sotheby's <u>global luxury home's report.</u>

Put simply, at 72.1 million, millennials are the largest generation with unique buying preferences. These priorities have profoundly influenced the direction and path of the housing market.

Market-moving preferences have seen a great shift as more educated, and qualified millennials have shown a strong interest in multifamily rentals. They have a relatively higher earning potential, and that is why they are all set to take over more than their prior generation.

This may sound strange to you, but millennial preferences are driven by their environmentally conscious and tech-savvy values. These dynamic preferences have dramatically shaped the housing market, particularly during the pandemic.

Beginning immediately after the pandemic, many buyers, for instance, flocked to places that offer walkability, high quality of life. It clearly shows that when it comes to investing in the multifamily real estate business, millennials are the main tenants. As they first think about their overall style of living, it propelled the second-tier markets into millennia's interest list.

Moving forward, another reason why millennials have become a strong buying force of multifamily real estate is that they like to incorporate high-tech features into their homes. This is one way to bolster sustainability in new houses.

That means when it comes to permanent changes, most multifamily apartment complexes are equipped with solar panels, green panels, and energy-saving geothermal systems, making them more attractive for millennials.

So, if you invest in a multifamily building that is environmentally friendly and move-in ready, with an installed garage, they generate an excellent premium, you will have many buyers competing for the rentals. Overall, the modern real estate market is quite ripe for revenue growth.

Urban Renaissance Became a Positive Driver for Multifamily Demand

In most urban areas in the US, the residential and commercial landscape is evolving to address and respond to the preferences and priorities of the population focused on different multifamily housing with conveniences, social engagement, and amenities.

Considering that Generation Z is the most active buyer or tenant of multifamily units, it is not surprising that the demand for modern homes in the urban sector is higher than traditional properties.

In fact, many surveys show most people prefer a detached property. Contemporary architectural design is also one of the most desired choices, and many prefer colonial. Interestingly, many millennials wish to live in the suburbs with scenic locations and waterfronts in urban locations. They also like a place close to dining venues, restaurants, other entertainment areas, and outdoor spaces with dedicated home offices.

Truly, an educated and modern buyer wants to "have-it-all." But keep in mind that urban renaissance is not only about buying bigger properties. People need an estate with a smaller footprint, amenities which are highly attractive. Getting the best out of your multifamily real estate investment is only possible when you know how to stand out and keep customers for life.

Let's make the process easier for you. Here is how you can use urban renaissance as a positive driver for your multifamily apartment building.

Expand Your Knowledge of Your Location's Inventory

Knowing your multifamily units inside out is pivotal if you want to expand your real estate business. You should know when a property is sold, to whom, for how many dollars, and what its strong features were.

Since the modern home or multifamily housing market is typically large, tour each unit. If you don't want to hire an agent, make sure to note the unique features of all the units. It will help you make a well-informed decision and master the selling strategies.

Be Visible

Most buyers don't spend much time browsing real estate websites and social media to find an ideal home. To attract and retain clients, casting the net where your potential clients hang out is the key.

How about socializing and spending time gathering where high-paying clients are?

It is important to know your client on a personal level. When you're out at family events or meeting new people, get to know those around you. Whatever you do, do not go and ask people if they know anybody that wants to buy or sell a home.

Instead, get to know them personally and show interest in their life, occupation, family, dreams, etc. Eventually, they'll be so interested in who you are and they'll want to know more about you and what you have to offer.

In addition to that, you can consider organizing a home staging to attract more buyers or tenants to your apartment building. A well-staged multifamily property enables potential tenants to ensure that the building meets all their needs, including layout, design, amenities, and structural standpoint.

They look for signs showing the condition of the units, parking, and neighborhood space of the building house. If the units in your multifamily property are properly-staged, they can create a great impression on your prospective tenants and buyers.

You can also host a housewarming party to be more visible to buyers. This is a great way to develop a friendly relationship with them. Get printed invitations, custom paper napkins, coasters, snacks, and beverages. It's ideal for greeting neighbors who might be your prospective clients.

Moreover, personally helping clients by buying from them is another good idea to make prospecting easy. For instance, if your client owns a car wash business, you can hire their services and give your vehicle a rinse at their establishment. Or, if they run a catering company, book them for your next event.

Speak in the buyer's language, and don't get carried away with real estate jargon and things that don't make sense to your average multifamily buyer or tenant. Create massive value for your buyers by solving their problems (i.e., help them navigate purchase within a short period or make them feel good (i.e., find them their dream home).

Deal with them by seeking to understand your buyers' or tenants' pain points and then set them on the right path.

These are some easy ways to reach out to the maximum number of people to promote your multifamily real estate business.

Consider Testimonials

You must meet the demands of buyers for successful marketing. The best thing about modern, urban and potential customers is that they like to be published. That means you can find them in different testimonials and reviews. Use it as a golden opportunity and browse through their comments to see what they are looking for.

Don't forget that a large percentage of people who look for an urban lifestyle are high-end clients. A high-end client is an ideal buyer for a company or firm looking to close a deal. These types of clients often look for unique homes and don't mind paying extra.

Many agents mistake these clients with some DIVA clients who are too irrational and demanding. They are not the ideal clients one can aim for.

Preferential Mortgage Market

As said above, financing institutes and lenders feel safer when financing a multi-family property. It is because the type of real estate business distributes the risk of investment across more than one unit instead of just one. Plus, multifamily properties tend to hold value for a longer period.

According to the Real Capital Analytic's study, a multifamily investor has better opportunities and financing terms. If you have a multifamily building with two to six units and is owner-occupied, you may obtain leverage of 95 percent and 96.5 percent from some lenders.

This is a great advantage over single-family real estate lending that allows owners to leverage between 70 percent and 75 percent. Moreover, the loans for an owner-occupied multifamily building get a better interest rate, which is typically 3 percent lower than any commercial loan.

Put simply, many inventors purchase real estate to earn a return via cash flow. If the investment is set on a single property that remains vacant for three months, you will not have any income from the unit during this period.

Also, you still have to pay for your expenses and mortgage. But it is different when you have a multifamily property. As the risk of vacancies is distributed among several units or tenants, it substantially decreases the risk of receiving no income for months.

Tax Incentives

There are many tax incentives a multifamily property owner can take advantage of. Note that tax makes a large portion of your overall expenses that different types of rental units incur. Plus, there is no way you can skip this mandatory levy. If you evade paying your taxes, you will break the law.

But when it comes to multifamily properties, there are tips you can use to reduce these tax obligations. Multifamily properties also have a fair share of income tax breaks.

If you know how to use them, it could make all the difference between saving and paying thousands every year.

Here are some tricks.

Depreciation Tax Benefits

Depreciation is the best and perhaps biggest tax shelter for a multifamily property owner. It is based on the principle that units depreciate over time. Thus, the depreciation amount can be a tax deduction to cover the wear and tear of the property over the years. It is worth mentioning that the IRS treats houses like assets.

Like other valuables, the quality of real estate also diminishes over the years. In reality, it rarely happens because many property owners keep up with the maintenance. And an expanding neighborhood also improves the value of the property.

It is worth mentioning that whether your apartment complex makes profits or appreciates, you can claim your depreciation expenses as a deductible on your income tax return. It means as a multifamily real estate investor, tax depreciation can offer you a massive tax break.

Wondering how does it work?

Let's understand.

The Internal Revenue Service allows residential and commercial real estate investors in the US to reduce the value of their investment properties in equal installments over a period of 27 and 39 years, respectively. Thus, the IRS allows property owners or landlords to deduct or subtract a depreciation expense for a specific period.

To estimate the depreciation amount of a property, you need to divide its cost by the number of useful years. For instance, if your apartment building is worth $500,000, it will have an annual depreciation expense of around $18,518:

$$$500,000/27$$

Let's admit, subtracting such a huge amount from your multifamily building's taxable income will save you a lot. If your property generates $80,000 per year, you will have a tax obligation of:

Tax without depreciation:

$$$80,000 \times 25 \text{ percent} = $20,000$$

Taxes owed with depreciation:

($80,000 – $18,518) x 25 percent = $15,370

Thus, in these scenarios, you will get to save around $4,629 per year without including or adding any deductions. Isn't it amazing?

What Else?

Interestingly, tax depreciation is not the only taxation benefit you get from a multi-family real estate business. 1031 Exchange is another way to save on your taxable investment property.

Fortunately, the IRS code section 1031 has made it possible for investors to defer paying taxes on selling an investment property if they buy a "similar property" with the proceeds they get from the old property. The strategy reduces the tax burden on multifamily real estate investors.

How Does 1031 Work?

Section 1031 applies when a real estate investor swaps an investment property with another similar property. To make this work, in the 1031 exchange, a QI or accommodator works as a facilitator to hold the proceeds received from the sale of the old property. The facilitator uses the proceeds to purchase its replacement for an investor. After that, the IRS treats this exchange as a swap.

Normally, when someone sells an investment property, they have to pay capital gain taxes. This can make selling properties a burden and even result in poor investment returns. However, if you have a multifamily rental property that has increased in value compared to its original purchase price, you can re-invest those potential profits.

The tax-deferred strategy works effectively when purchasing a property with the same value. The strategy helps you avoid the capital gain tax that would otherwise be applied to the sale transaction.

Essentially, you have to consider these steps for a 1031 exchange:

- Selling an investment property
- Handing capital gains on the sold property to any qualified intermediary
- Identifying a similar property in less than 45 days

But you need the assistance of a professional, qualified intermediary to help you complete the process. It can be either a company or a person who facilitates the receipt and deployment of 1031 exchange funds. They are responsible for holding the funds used in the property transaction. They hold the funds until they transfer them to the seller of the replacement property.

In short, if you're a multifamily real estate investor, consider using 1031 exchange, especially if you want to purchase a property with a better potential for returns or you want to diversify your assets.

As an investor, you can also use this tax benefit if you want to outsource property management and do not want to manage them yourself or are considering consolidating many properties in one for further estate planning.

Way, this structured strategy allows multifamily real estate investors to reinvest into new properties and defer the capital gain.

Real Estate Investment Tax Deduction

Another easy way to reduce the tax burden on your multifamily business is to benefit from tax deductions. So, what does tax deduction mean?

There are several rental property tax deductions that owners can use in order to reduce and even eliminate their taxable rental income. As a property owner, this law allows you to subtract the expenses incurred from total taxable income to repair and maintain your apartment building.

In general, one way to decrease your tax obligation is to write off property maintenance expenses from your taxable income. These expenses may include:

- Insurance premiums
- Maintenance or repair expenses
- Management costs
- Utilities
- Mortgage interest
- Marketing costs

Obviously, the lower your taxable earnings, the lower your tax burden.

Short-Term Lease Allows You to Adapt to Market Conditions

Most multifamily buildings or complexes are on yearly or monthly rental leases. However, other rental properties, including retail stores, and offices are on a lease of five years. It is a tremendous advantage for multifamily assets.

We say this because short-term leases allow multifamily property owners to adjust rents according to market conditions.

With short-term leases, real estate investors have more flexibility to increase the rent if the housing market is flourishing. This way, they can get high rental returns. It makes short-term leases or month-to-month leases particularly convenient and profitable.

Put simply, if your apartment building or multifamily property needs flexibility, you can draft your lease agreement accordingly. It will not be a full-year contract and allows you to tailor your lease based on your timing requirements, reducing worry and stress. If you want to terminate the lease or exit the contract early, you will incur fewer penalties.

You always have an option to switch to a long-term lease if you like your multifamily property or it is profiting you more than you expected. Keep in mind that a short-term lease gives you the ability to change the contract terms at the time of renewal.

For instance, if you want to change or update the security deposit terms, pet policy, or inspection requirement, you can easily do it by entering into a new lease contract with your tenant.

If you usually rent out your apartment units to people who are in the town for a temporary period or need a vacation rental, a short-term lease is an ideal way to benefit from the contract. In fact, you can charge a higher rent from your tenants during the peak season.

Did you know that in many jurisdictions, annual leases automatically turn into a monthly lease once the contract expires? It remains the same unless property owners and tenants sign a new contract or lease agreement.

Whether it is about changing terms in the contract or charging high rent, the short-term lease can benefit a multi-family real estate business in many ways. But you must know that it may have its downside. This is especially true if the economic conditions change. Short lease tenures can also result in a faster decline in rental prices.

CHAPTER 4
INVESTING STRATEGIES

Now, as you know how a multifamily business can help you reap tons of economic benefits, we suggest investing in real estate is an excellent idea to increase your wealth. In fact, when it comes to long-term financial security, there is no better option.

If your cash flow is steady, multifamily real estate investing brings many financial benefits for a long time. For example, if you own an apartment complex, it offers you a sense of security as the property's value appreciates over time. That means your property's value will increase as both buildings and land are appreciating assets.

Another benefit of multifamily real estate that makes it an ideal investment is that it acts as a hedge against price increases. Know that if the inflation rate is high, the property value and rental income increase significantly. That is why all real estate investors make a lot of money during inflation because their cash flow increases.

Don't forget the tax exemptions we have talked about in the last chapter that set multifamily real estate investing apart from other investment options. Many investors invest in properties to get long-term financial benefits without paying any taxes.

For instance, there is no self-employment tax on your rental income. The government's tax breaks for maintenance repairs, property depreciation, insurance, travel expenses, property taxes, and legal fees are great to keep ROI steady. Besides this, real estate investors pay lower tax rates for all the long-term investments, which are like the icing on the cake!

Plus, the rental income you receive monthly from your multifamily building is enough to pay your expenses, including your mortgage payments. You can make your tenants pay the mortgage just by keeping them happy and mitigating the negative consequences of vacancy at any cost.

To reiterate, merely saving money in banks can never benefit you financially in the long run, nor does it maximize your wealth. You must have a reliable investment option, and a multifamily real estate business offers you plenty of investing benefits, such as steady income, long-standing financial security, and tax benefits.

But you definitely need some effective strategies to make your investment in real estate successful. In this chapter, we will discuss some of the most useful and beneficial investment strategies, along with their benefits and uses.

Value-Add (BRRRR)

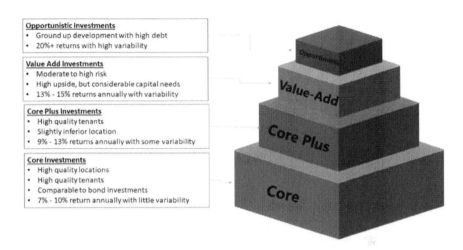

Opportunistic Investments
- Ground up development with high debt
- 20%+ returns with high variability

Value Add Investments
- Moderate to high risk
- High upside, but considerable capital needs
- 13% - 15% returns annually with variability

Core Plus Investments
- High quality tenants
- Slightly inferior location
- 9% - 13% returns annually with some variability

Core Investments
- High quality locations
- High quality tenants
- Comparable to bond investments
- 7% - 10% return annually with little variability

Source: https://bullpenre.com/core-core-plus-value-add-opportunistic/

Buy

Buying and holding a long-term property as a real estate investment strategy works best if you know the right marketing and leasing tactics. It is better to consult a professional to find out more about the best leasing strategies or creative funding strategies that will help you finance the multifamily building you're interested in buying.

"Buy and hold" is a popular investment strategy that involves purchasing a property to be held for many years. It is a popular strategy partly because of the ease of acquiring a buy-and-hold property. Many buy-and-hold investors become investors by circumstances.

Inheriting a property and moving out of the one you can't sell are two popular ways of becoming an accidental real estate investor. If you choose this strategy with a well-designed structure to invest in your multifamily real estate business, it can help you build wealth over time.

Do you want to learn how the "buy and hold" real estate strategy works?

As said above, the buy and hold is a long-term investing strategy that works well for passive investments. It is simpler than other real estate tactics. All you need to do is buy a multifamily property and hold onto it for a long time. You can hold an apartment building for decades. Make sure you look for multifamily units with the potential for stable cash flow and appreciation.

Typically, property prices fluctuate according to the market conditions. Savvy investors look for opportunities to purchase at low prices to make more profit. Still, using a buy-and-hold strategy in the multifamily real estate business assumes that the asset will increase in value.

Many investors buy and hold a multifamily apartment building for the foreseeable future. However, if you're looking to finance a real estate purchase, the rates you get may vary depending on when you buy.

Multifamily real estate investors who want to purchase without an all-cash deal must keep an eye on the interest rates. It helps them shop around or find the best option. It is also important to calculate the income potential of your apartment building when using a buy-and-hold strategy. If you're financing your purchase for investment, you need to put down at least 20 percent of the total purchase price of the property.

A buy and hold strategy for a multifamily real estate business has less volatility and predictable cash flow than the volatile stock market. You can also benefit from the Opportunity Zones program. The zones are areas that the Tax Cuts and Jobs Act of 2017 has created. The designated regions allow real estate investors to purchase properties in lower-income and distressed areas to get tax advantages.

When Selling a Buy-And-Hold Investment Property is the Best Option

Ideally, you can hold onto your investment property for 5 to 10 years. This period may increase, depending on the market conditions. However, if you're considering selling, you may want to consider the following.

- **Tax Breaks**- Tax code advantages work great for investors looking to sell the multifamily property and purchase another to avoid capital gains taxes.

- **Loan Term**- If the loan term has ended, it is the right time to sell your investment property.

- **Favorable market conditions**- Keep yourself updated with the value of comparable buildings in the housing market. If the value increases, it is a seller's market. You can put your property for sale, so you don't have to wait for the next cycle.

- **Increasing property taxes**- Increasing property taxes in the area can also be a sign that you should consider selling your multifamily property to avoid higher rates.

Benefits of a Buy and Hold Investment Strategy

Your real estate portfolio comprises a set of investment assets. Buying and holding a multifamily building is an effective strategy to make money. The property generates a consistent cash flow as passive income. The steady income from your multifamily real estate business can help you make the mortgage payment on the properties. In fact, a real estate portfolio diversifies risk with each investment you make.

Rehabbing

Rehabbing is all about making simple or extensive renovations to the property. You can spruce up your multifamily property by repainting the exterior.

If you decide to purchase an apartment building in a modern neighborhood, you are typically banking on that neighborhood to increase in value. Buying in the newly constructed locality means you might not necessarily renovate the units. You also find high-end buyers who want the modern and advanced features and spaces in the suburbs.

On the other hand, if the multifamily property you buy needs major renovations, it may drain your wallet. This is when you need the right skills and strategies to find the right property with minimum rehabbing requirements.

However, the given tips can help you find the best multifamily investment option for rehab.

Become a Member of Real Estate Investment Groups

Numerous areas have local investment groups that provide people with networking opportunities. They frequently list real estate opportunities on various websites or newsletters. That gives group members access to excellent investment advice.

The groups may have several referral networks for multifamily rehabbers where they can help members find properties to buy. For example, NationalReia.org is a good place to find suitable investing groups. It provides a comprehensive list of real estate investing groups in different states.

These groups also offer information on seminars, educational newsletters, and online questioning sessions to help real estate members understand this business. It helps them maximize real estate opportunities in the area.

These groups are worth joining no matter what your experience level is in the multifamily real estate business. You will be able to find which houses or properties you can rehab and rent.

Team up with a Wholesaler

Teaming up with a wholesaler can be a good idea to find the right multifamily property to buy and rehab. A wholesaler is a person who finds a rehab property, puts it under contract, and then finds a potential buyer for it.

The wholesaler essentially makes repairs under the contract instead of the buyer and pays a fee for working as a middleman. It may seem an expensive method to find a rehab property, but it is quite efficient and can save you a great deal of time and money.

For many wholesalers, flipping properties is a full-time job. They are familiar with different neighborhoods, sellers, and agents in the area. In general, you can find wholesalers on various real estate investments forums and groups, and you can search them through the internet.

Hire REO Specialists or Real Estate Agents

Many properties go through a lengthy foreclosure process if the owners would not leave. Most often, the last occupants who stayed in the property did no or little property maintenance during their eviction and foreclosure period.

As a result, the property remains neglected, which reduces its prices below the market value. But that is a good sign for you.

Many loan servicers and lenders align themselves with a group of real estate agents that specialize in finding and selling distressed properties. You can find these low-priced properties by working with these realtors.

They keep track of new rehab properties and real estate listing on the market. You can easily find these agents by searching on the internet for "REO" and "REO brokers" within your specific geographic location. They will help you find the best properties that need minor rehab.

Search the Neighborhood You Want to Purchase

Driving around the neighborhoods where you want to buy a multifamily property is a good idea to begin your search. Many expert rehabbers do this to locate potential properties they wish to buy.

Generally, investors pick a property that is typical and rugged in construction style compared to its neighborhood, showing clear signs of neglected maintenance. After that, they search the property's land records to find its owner and reach out to him via mail or phone with a purchase offer.

This method has a success rate even though many owners are not interested in selling the property. They take the offer as an opportunity to sell it in the future.

Find Rehab Properties on the Internet

There are plenty of lists on the internet that enumerate short sales, distressed properties, and foreclosures. Depending on the location, these lists are sorted by towns, cities, or zip codes. These lists can be an excellent resource for finding the right multifamily property that needs improvement.

Although these lists are usually free, some sources sell these lists to people interested in finding distressed properties. You can begin with the free lists to find the apartment buildings within your budget.

With the current news sources, finding lists of profitable rehab projects has become quite convenient. Lists like ClassicProperties.com and BankForeclosedListings.com are a few examples available on the internet to help you find the right rehab properties.

What to Remember?

For many individuals, rehabbing houses is a full-time job. They make significant returns on investments. Plus, when you regularly purchase homes and materials for renovation, it also helps you develop negotiating skills. You learn to delegate tasks, deal with money matters, and manage time effectively. These skills can be used in different kinds of businesses.

Rehabbing may include owners who buy and renovate houses for personal use or keep them until property value increases. Natural appreciation helps you make money or build wealth without putting in any effort. It is a good way to make some short-term money. But it can only happen if the multifamily property is in good shape and doesn't require repairs and major fixes.

You need to be smart and vigilant in your property investment plans, especially when finding a multifamily building to rehab. You might have to employ many methods to find the property that is right for you.

Moreover, when you buy real estate properties and hold on to them, it allows you to expand your investment portfolio easily.

Make an Outline with Details and Specifics for Rehab Project

Once you assess the property's condition, you need to make an outline. This outline covers the scope of work your rehab needs. It heavily relies on how well your pre-rehab planning is.

To perform this task efficiently, you should:

- List all repairs and renovation needed (e.g., floor installations, demolitions, removals, etc.)
- Budget efficiently
- Estimate the total cost

When to Advertise

Your timing in advertising decides the fate of your property. Staging the property after completion of all the improvement work will help you maximize the profits.

Multifamily Rehabbing- Plan a Deeper Value-Add

Most multifamily buildings that are for sale have gone through some renovation. However, as an investor, you must find out if there is a need for more. An old apartment building can be one of these:

- Fully renovated
- Partially renovated
- Untouched

Untouched: If a multifamily property is untouched, it is a great opportunity primed for rental upside and capital investment. But if the building is located with other comparable units in the vicinity that doesn't justify rental upside, it may not benefit you.

Partially Renovated: You should decide whether you want to continue executing the current owner's rehab plan on the remaining units. If the building has potential for value-add (better renovation), will you make the changes on the untouched units? Or on all units that already have undergone renovation recently?

Fully Renovated: How about revisiting all the units to see if they need new/better improvements? Sometimes there is great room for improvement even if the property was recently renovated. The partially renovated properties are the trickiest to make improvements.

Understanding the high-level state of the units is easy. But planning for the actual logistics involved in a renovation with different rehab plans and costs can be challenging.

Let's help you make this decision easily. Here is what you can do to plan rehab for units after taking over the building's ownership.

Organization

Reliable and accurate information about the current state of your multi-family property is essential. Contact a property manager who is overseeing the building. It will help you find out:

- Number of units in the property
- Each unit's floor plan
- Each unit's details with square footage

- Each unit's rent
- Implemented updates/improvements in each unit

You don't always get records of multifamily rehabs from the property management company. Some property managers do rehabs randomly and don't file the document.

If this happens to you, make detailed notes and take pictures when visiting the units. It may seem annoying, but it can be a valuable opportunity.

Once you figure out which units have undergone renovation and what those updates are, develop a business plan.

Pre-Planning

Some of the most crucial assumptions that are relevant when you make a business plan include:

- What improvements are needed?
- How expensive can these updates be?
- What rental capital they can generate

If you're thinking about upgrading lighting, carpets, installing appliances, and hard surfaces, look for comparable properties that have made similar improvements. See if these changes have increased the rental income. But a comparable property should have:

- Similar amenities
- A similar location
- Construction year

You can also check out the new construction in different sub-markets. It provides investors with fantastic property improvement ideas. It is easy to mimic the changes and features of the latest developments in your older property.

The idea to implement up-to-date features can work well even if you have budget-conscious renters. Also, it is one way to reduce the cost difference between your multifamily building and the newer competitions.

Practical Obsolescence

Sometimes, when you redevelop a distressed multifamily building, some outdated components make it hard to achieve maximum rents upon rehab completion. These examples include:

- 8-ft ceilings
- Outdated floor plans
- No underground parking
- No communal amenity space

If you think your value-add strategy can compete with the new constructions, you're mistaken. If your value-add multifamily building lacks a parking area, includes 8 feet ceilings, has limited closet space, and has a closed-off floor plan, it will not get the rent comparable to new constructions.

Even if your property matches the finish levels, you cannot change the ceiling height of the units. The units with an 8 feet ceiling feel claustrophobic and smaller than new projects. Nowadays, new constructions have floor-to-ceiling windows that make the space look bigger.

Moreover, it is difficult to achieve the convenience of a secured parking space. You may try to move or remove some walls or partitions to make outdated units look spacious. But they will never get the same feel as the new constructions you're competing against.

Business Plan

Once you have a bigger picture of rehabs in your apartment building, it is time to focus on other details that include:

- The cost of the updates for the unit's floor-plan (for previously renovated and old units)
- How many units can you rehab each month?
- The time you begin the value-add execution
- How long do you have to keep the units vacant while upgrading? Four weeks? Six weeks?
- The average ROI (**return on investment**) for your renovation plan

These points vary depending on the strategy you use. For example, if your apartment building has 80 units and is a 1970's construction, you need to make the following improvements:

- New Cabinets
- Laminate Flooring
- Black Appliances
- Energy-efficient Plumbing Fixtures
- Lighting Fixtures

Renovating each unit with these upgrades may take a month. Ideally, you will be able to renovate 20 to 30 units a month.

Rent

Monthly rentals are your traditional residential lease agreements that involve renting a designated space for a fixed amount each month. However, buying a multifamily rental property for the first time raises many concerns and questions.

You don't buy properties every day, and that makes it a significant financial decision in your life. You need to be sure that the multifamily property you want to invest in is a profitable investment.

So, before you make this decision, ask yourself these questions to develop a foundation for your first multifamily investment property.

How can I find a lucrative multifamily investment property?

The first thing you need to consider when buying a multifamily rental property is your financial goals. You must find a rental property that suits your budget and can help you make a profit.

You can choose a traditional route. Look at published ads for multifamily properties or contact an experienced agent to find the best option. Browsing the internet for searching lucrative opportunities is also a good idea. Check reliable websites such as Trulia and Realtor.com.

How can I evaluate if a multifamily rental property is a worthwhile investment?

You can determine the investment value by calculating its cash flow. You must understand how much cash flow a rental property generates before signing a deal. Deduct the monthly expenses from the rental income to determine the cash flow. If you have more cash flow, that means the property is a worthwhile investment.

What options can I use to finance my property purchase?

Check your finances before you finalize the deal for your multifamily rental deal. You should have a high credit score to obtain a loan. Lenders check the credit score to ensure you can make the monthly payments. You should have a credit score between 600 and 640 to obtain the loan.

If you have suitable credit scores, plan how you will finance your first rental property. You can choose different ways to finance the multifamily property. However, it depends on your investment aspiration, time, and goals.

Do I need to hire a real estate agent?

A real estate agent can perform several essential duties for buying a rental property. He helps you get pre-approved for home loans, assesses the housing market, negotiate deals, deal with property appraisals, and close the deal.

These tasks are time-consuming when you don't have a real estate agent. If you want to avoid this complex process, hire the services of a professional agent to make your monthly rental investment a success. He will deal with challenging parts of the process. He can also assist you in documentation and renovation.

A multifamily rental property makes an ideal investment if chosen smartly. It has helped many first-time investors generate a consistent income and grow their real estate business. However, you must know how to evaluate monthly rentals before investing.

As an investor, you can profit from two sources:

- Monthly rental income

- Appreciation of property

You can evaluate monthly rental investments in a multifamily property using the capitalization rate formula, also known as the cap rate. The cap rate is found by taking the Net Operating Income (NOI) and dividing it by the property value or purchase price.

Take gross rents or potential rents and subtract all expenses. This includes taxes, insurance, and expected repairs.

Refinance

Yes, it is possible to refinance your commercial loan after achieving 80 percent to 85 percent occupancy in your multifamily business. Did you know that your commercial lender allows you to cash out more than 75 percent of the current valuation of the property? This is true when you:

- Renovate the property
- Increase rents from your existing tenants
- Lower your operating costs

Not sure how refinancing your multifamily property can benefit you? Here are some advantages.

Low-Interest Rate

A low-interest rate is the biggest benefit of refinancing a multifamily property. If you're planning to hold onto the investment property for two to three years, refinancing your commercial loan into a new financing credit with a new interest will boost your cash flow. It decreases out-of-pocket costs on the investment property.

Rates with a reliable multifamily program go as low as 8 percent based on:

- Property's value-add rehab requirements
- The stability of the housing market
- Refinancing to leverage equity

Explore cash-out refinance options to leverage the equity into your multifamily property. It is a good strategy to cash out more than 60 percent of the loan-to-value (worth as-is) of the property if it is stabilized.

This is a great option for many investors as it allows them to use the cash from the property and purchase more properties. It is an easy way to grow your multifamily real estate business.

Refinancing for Renovation/Rehab Funds

Refinancing a multifamily building allows you to acquire rehab funds. That means when you buy the multifamily units, you can recapitalize up to 70 percent of the ARV loan (After Repair Value). It is equal to the worth of the property once the renovation is complete. It helps you acquire the funds necessary to complete the rehab.

Rehab completion increases the value of the property. It allows investors to hold onto it for at least two years with extension time available before selling the building or refinancing it for a long term.

These benefits of refinancing the multifamily property help you capitalize on your asset. They provide funds to complete value-added renovation to the units, which can increase the property's value. In turn, you have a better monthly cash flow.

Repeat

Now you're familiar with the entire process. It is time to grow your real estate investment portfolio using your profits. You have sufficient initial cash and can invest it in other multifamily complexes.

Opportunistic

An opportunistic strategy is considered the riskiest real estate tactic. It mimics the characteristics of "stock market growth." But it can be even riskier if you're not an experienced investor. As an opportunistic multifamily real estate investor, you take on complicated projects and invest in them. You might not get any return on your investment for two to three years.

It is always better to work with professional realtors who have significant experience using opportunistic investment strategies. They can help you acquire an empty building, ground-up developments, maintain land development, and reposition a building.

Opportunistic properties have little cash flow at the beginning. But once value-add rehabs are complete, the properties can generate a great amount of cash flow. In fact, an opportunistic investor tends to leverage more than 70 percent of the investment. However, this amount of leverage varies depending on the debt investors can obtain.

For instance, banks and other financial institutes will not lend more than 40 percent. Opportunistic investors can obtain more than 20 percent annual returns for their real estate investment.

Stages of an Opportunistic Investment for Multifamily Real Estate Business

Most opportunistic projects comprise the same process, including asset purchasing and its sale. However, each phase comes with its considerations and risks. Investors need to pay attention to each specific outlined in the potential investment plan.

Check out these three stages that require your vigilance when making an opportunistic investment.

Pre-Development

Investors need to get approval for many projects before the construction starts. This process includes securing zoning, environmental testing, government permits, and obtaining building approvals. The pre-development stage is typically the riskiest stage of this type of project investment.

Development

With the necessary approvals, the investors begin working with engineers, architects, and contractors. They use pre-leasing at this stage that gives the project enough time to reach the break-even point and achieve a state of steady cash flow (stabilization).

Lease-Up and Stabilization

Once the apartment building is complete and ready for occupants, it is time to start leasing to potential tenants. When the multifamily building achieves full occupancy, the investor either sells the property for profit or refinances with new debt.

Exit

The last stage is for estimating a three to five-year holding period. The period is between the beginning of an opportunistic investment project and its sale. An investment can hold short periods up to one year to make estimations.

Many experts group multifamily real estate investment opportunities into four profiles. These usually start with the least risky along the risk-reward scale and end with the riskier called "opportunistic" profile.

A business plan plays an important role in determining where your opportunistic investment falls on the risk-reward scale. However, as you move forward on the risk-reward scale, your chances of getting significant gains or compensation improve.

That means, if you're ready to take on the challenges and additional risks, opportunistic investments can add to your portfolio. It pays you off better than other real estate strategies.

Here are the deals you can get in an opportunistic investment strategy.

Heavy Value-Add

Opportunistic properties require significant rehabilitation to realize their full potential. Often these assets are fully vacant at the acquisition date. As an operator, you may need to develop the land from the ground up.

Land Assemblage

Land assemblage is another tactic for land acquisition. You can acquire multiple adjacent parcels and combine them into one. Remember that the process might get difficult if you have many parcels.

Land Banking

Land banking is a great strategy you can use for your multifamily real estate business by converting properties into economic development. You need to maintain, demolish, or sell the land for redeveloping. You can gain profits with the increase in the property's value over time.

Land Development

A land development strategy integrates overall spatial planning with sectoral, financial, and institutional planning. It encourages the expansion of land when major infrastructure networks around the property improve.

Core

Core investment is considered the least risky as it targets fully leased, secure, and stabilized investments in the main core markets. It may include properties with a long-term lease to Class A buildings and credit tenants in desirable locations. The building complex is usually kept upscale and needs little improvement.

This is one reason why properties of this type don't appreciate much. But they provide predictable, stable cash flow with relatively low risk. The investment type suits investors looking for long holding periods and capital preservation. Plus, it offers low leverage acquisition.

While you may find this investment type less attractive if you compare it to higher-yielding real estate opportunities, it is an attractive investment for many investors for its low-risk level.

It is especially true when you compare it with other investment opportunities in the market, including publically traded equities and bonds.

Characteristics of Core Investments

Located within Primary (Major) Markets

A core multifamily complex can be a recently built luxury apartment or a tower with a relatively low vacancy in major markets.

Fully Leased Assets

The core investments are fully leased because they have credit tenants. Regardless of the type of property you have, you can purchase it with less than 40 percent debt.

High-Credit Tenant Base

Typically, core investment has credit tenants on long-term leases with reliable and solid guarantors, such as Walgreen or Starbucks. Most multifamily core investments are within the best locations of town. The properties need no improvements.

Core investments are safer than bonds and have higher returns because of the higher tenant demand.

Class A or Trophy Buildings

Core investment is primarily for Class A properties in high-quality locations with elite and wealthy tenants. They rent or purchase it with little or no debt. The properties have a low-risk profile. You can even compare it to equity investment or bond investment opportunities.

You may find many life insurance companies, hedge funds, and other investment groups using this strategy. It is because they look for stable cash flow that can help them preserve capital.

Core Plus

A core plus real estate investment strategy seeks high-quality renters in good but not excellent locations. Note that most core plus units are slightly lower quality than core properties. Investors purchase them aggressively using more debt.

The cash flow with these properties is more variable. However, it has the potential to generate high returns. That means you can expect at least 9 percent to 13 percent annualized returns. Some of the upsides in core-plus real estate may include:

- Cosmetic improvements, such as painting exterior/ interior, new flooring
- Hiring a property manager
- Recruiting a leasing team

As mentioned above, these properties have higher cap rates than core properties. Also, they tend to have higher vacancy rates and risks.

Stabilized Assets

A stabilized asset is any property that doesn't need any renovation or construction. Plus, the property reaches a certain occupancy rate (90 percent of the units). It achieves a stable net operating income, supporting debt services. As an incoming operator, you need all the operations running to keep consistent cash flow.

With no construction delays or stoppages, the stabilized assets can operate for significantly low rates.

Trophy Assets

This range of real estate products is from the most coveted category, with Trophy assets being the latest segment. In real estate, a trophy asset refers to a property in high demand and exceptionally rare. It can be the largest development or the tallest building within the housing market.

You may find these assets in the best locations, which offer easy access and exceptional visibility with strong demand from renters. Investors hold these assets for higher rental rates and long-term capital appreciation. Trophy assets can help you achieve these goals by changing liquid assets into a secure investment to get consistent cash flow.

CHAPTER 5
WHERE TO PUT MONEY

Top 3 Tips for Investing in a Specific Property

Find Your 50%

A comprehensive analyzer of your multifamily real estate business deal is crucial for your investment. You need a quick system that serves as an initial evaluation for your potential property. You can assess a multifamily deal even with limited information with the calculation like the 50 % rule. The unique way of calculation determines whether your multifamily building is worth more effort and time.

Don't know what the 50% rule is, how it can work for your multifamily real estate business, and WHY adding this calculation to the toolkit is the right thing to do? Keep scrolling.

What Is The 50% Rule?

The 50% rule serves as a guideline for multifamily real estate investors. They use it to calculate the profitability and revenues of their rental units. As the title suggests, the 50%

rule involves taking away half of the rental income of a property when estimating its potential profits.

According to this rule, real estate investors should designate 50% of the rental income to expenses. They should not consider this income when comparing property's potential profits against loan repayments and monthly mortgage.

Though the rule is simple, involving some basic calculations, it helps multifamily real estate investors make informed decisions and realistic estimations. Many property investors underestimate the cost of expenses when searching for profitable deals.

This is a common mistake that reduces the profit margins or may result in an unsuccessful deal altogether. Incorporating a 50% rule into the calculations or initial review of the property deal is one way to protect it against unforeseen expenses and costs.

The rule has a simple mechanism to estimate the profit margins. Investors need to take the total rental income and divide it in half. It is to estimate the potential costs associated with buying or owning a multifamily building. The expenses are generally related to property management, repairs, and taxes. Remember that you don't need to know the accurate costs to use the 50% rule.

In fact, the calculation is a tried and tested way many multifamily real estate investors use to make a ballpark figure of the costs that come with potential deals with limited information. Note that that 50% rule doesn't classify loan payments and mortgages as expenses.

It is better to compare loan payments to the remaining half of your rental income to estimate whether it's beneficial to move forward with the multifamily property or not.

Let's say you're looking at a multifamily building in your market with a monthly rental income of $4,000.

According to the 50% rule, it means $2,000 of the rental income will be used for expenses of the units. It leaves you with $2000 to evaluate compared with your loan payments. However, if you need to pay $1,200 as a monthly mortgage on the multifamily property, the investment will, in theory, cash-flow at $800 a month.

Once you have this estimate, it's easier to use the numbers to do a more thorough analysis of your multifamily property.

Wondering if the 50% rule is accurate?

The 50% rule isn't accurate but it is a good guideline for your first multifamily property evaluation. You shouldn't treat it as an entirely accurate illustration of expenses when estimating the profit margins. We say this because this is estimation is made at the first stage of your deal analysis.

Investors usually don't have all the relevant statistics on a multifamily property required to nail down the total expenses. Therefore, it is better to consider the 50% rule as a general guideline instead of a hard and fast rule. Most real estate investors find that this rule overestimates the total costs associated with a property.

It happens because not all multifamily properties have the same taxes, maintenance requirements, or HOA fees. The costs are not total half of the rental income in reality. It can turn into a pleasant surprise as you start digging deeper into the numbers.

Also, the 50% rule doesn't account for vacant units as you don't have any guarantee that you will find tenants for all apartments right away or year-round.

How You can Make Money with the 50% Rule in Multifamily Real Estate

Estimating numbers and making early calculations as a multifamily real estate business owner is perhaps the best thing you can do. You need to find the difference between your income and expenses to make profits.

If estimating these seems a difficult task or accessing information is hard, try the 50% rule. According to this rule, investors should estimate their operating cost to be 50% of total income (cost ratio of half income). The rule also takes into account the experience of real estate investors.

For instance, if your rental units make $40,000 annually in gross rents, you can assume that $20,000 of the income will go into the cost operation. It doesn't include the mortgage payment. Some costs of operations include:

- Property Insurance
- Maintenance/Repairs
- Property Taxes
- Property Management
- Utilities

Even if you self-manage your multifamily real estate business, include a professional property manager in the calculations. They have the experience and understanding of expected income as well as expenses.

Consider this rule as a starter with a comprehensive and full-course property analysis to follow. If your multifamily property passes this test, you can estimate other metrics to move forward. As said above, you should never use this rule as a final say when it comes to making an investment decision.

Instead, apply the rule to determine when you *shouldn't* invest. For instance, if the mortgage on an apartment building exceeds half of its rental income after running the numbers, investing in the deal might not be the right option.

It is vital to show due diligence before you take on any investment opportunity. If you want to apply the 50% rule to estimate the profits, know that it must go hand in hand with thorough rental property calculations.

Make sure you research the market, inquire about previous multifamily property owners, and evaluate each aspect of your investment property before signing the deal. In the meantime, count on the 50% deal to get a quick evaluation (first phase) of your potential options.

Calculate Your Cash Flow

No matter what impeccable model you choose to run your multifamily real estate business, or how many potential investors are willing to invest in your startup if you cannot manage the cash flow of your property, surviving in this industry will be challenging.

The US bank (a financial services company) in one of its prominent studies found that nearly 82 small real estate startups fail in their initial phases due to a lack of expertise in cash-flow management.

So, if you want to be a smart and successful multifamily real estate business owner, it is vital to focus on managing the cash flow. It will help your business survive in the mainstream real estate world, but also keep all the imminent danger at bay.

Before we get into the details of how calculating cash flow can keep your multifamily real estate business benefit you, let us quickly go through some of the common mistakes many property owners make that cause cash-flow problems.

Lack of Attention to Real Estate Business Expenses

As unexpected expenses disturb your household budget, they may do the same with your multifamily real estate business. Many unexpected expenses, including natural disasters, replacing technology, costly repairs of equipment, or overspending may lead your business to an unsustainable point. Though the expenses may seem small, the cash flow crunches due to them.

As the leader of your multifamily real estate business, you must take a vigorous look into ongoing expenses; especially cost structure to resolve this type of cash flow crisis. It is essential for real estate startups to pay attention to certain even small expenses. Many entrepreneurs only focus on the profits they are making but do not realize how much money goes back.

A rigorous process of structure is critically important to help multifamily real estate businesses track expenses on monthly basis.

Extra Tip: hire a business accountant for your multifamily real estate business to manage and track the cash flow generated from the units. The manager can also help you anticipate future challenges to position your real estate business in a better way.

Overestimating Your Profit Volumes

Regardless of the type of business you have, optimism is one of the key traits of successful entrepreneurship.

In fact, it is the best way to prevent work stress and teething trouble of startups from taking a toll on you. While optimism is necessary for any new business, it shouldn't be compromised with the objectivity of the business owners. The situation precisely can be bad for the cash flow problem. And it goes the same for the multifamily real estate business.

If your profit volume increases in a short period, it doesn't mean that they get double by the end of the year (unless *you have extra capital to invest in*). Expecting such things are a little unrealistic; especially when you're new in the real estate business.

This is where you need realistic and objective cash-flow forecasting that is based on real numbers. Using quantitative for casting method is a great way o track trends based on past revenue data of your real estate business. You can predict future revenues with objective intuitions to help your multifamily real estate business make a realistic projection of returns.

Impulse Spending in Startup Phase

Many entrepreneurs believe that "money makes money." The common belief can be true in many cases, but it may make business owners fall prey to overspending. And if it is the initial phase of the business, it can be potentially dangerous for cash-flow management. It is because not all small business expenses are of the same nature.

While many beneficial expenses will translate into the profitability of your multifamily real estate business in several measurable ways, there are advisors, managers, and consultants who are ready to take the capital your startup makes. That is what keeping eye on the cost-benefit ratio is extremely important for all expenses of your multifamily building.

For that, creating a realistic budget is always beneficial. Calculate the cost of every single unit, unexpected expenses, and impulse spending (that may come up).

Being Passive about Unpaid Rents

No doubt this can be the fastest cash-flow killer if you don't pay attention. Many real estate startups suffer because of the unpaid rents that lead them to a poor cash-flow situation.

Multifamily real estate business owners, who are not pro-active when it comes to collecting payments on time, often face dangerous cash-flow situations.

Small businesses with no solid late-payment collection policies and late-payment penalties suffer a lot. Know that if your tenants know that they will not be notified if rent is delayed, you will be the last person to get paid from their list.

That means setting out clear policies and penalties for late rents is crucial. Whether your multifamily real estate business is new or is an established one, make sure you discuss the rent policies with the tenant before you clinch a deal.

A good way to deal with the late rent payments is to include a 5% penalty after 5 days. You can also apply the rule of a work stoppage (HVAC, repairs, etc.) after a month.

Working without a Cash-Flow Budget

You're working with realistic expectations, have reined your multifamily business expenses, and make sure that your tenants pay you on time. These changes can do wonders for your multifamily real estate business success as well as long-term cash flow. However, if you don't track the day-to-day cash flow of your business, it may still find tight spots.

The role of the cash-flow statement is important in tracking revenue inflow and expenses outflow. A cash-flow statement helps multifamily property owners anticipate when their business will have more expenses than money coming in. Considering these scenarios it is always best to plan for tighter budgets and difficult times.

Multifamily real estate businesses can only guess at whether they will have enough money to face past dues and late payments without a cash-flow statement

Maintaining healthy cash flow is the key to keeping your real estate business on the success track. Overcoming the given causes of cash-flow problems will help your multifamily real estate business rise and shine.

So now you know what you **SHOULDN'T** do when it comes to managing cash flow, it's time to learn what you **SHOULD** do to calculate it.

Bring the estimated mortgage payments into the equation by calculating your estimated monthly cash flow. Find out how much money you'll be putting into your wallet by subtracting the monthly mortgage from the property's NOI.

Cash flow is a lifeline in the real estate business. Unlike the first step, when calculating your cash flow you need to take mortgage payments into account.

Calculate your monthly cash flow by:

- Determining the gross income from the multifamily property
- Deducting all operating costs relating to the units

- Subtracting debt services relating to the multifamily property

The difference is the cash flow of your property.

Figure Out Your Cap Rate

Capitalization rate or cap rate is an important metric real estate investors use to analyze their real estate investments. They use the metric to compare it with the cap rates of other properties with similar features. It is also a crucial number to evaluate the ROI and risk involved in property investment. It helps investors find the potential investment properties or evaluate if the current investment is being managed properly.

Why determining cap rate is crucial for your multifamily real estate investment?

Cap rate is a smart way to figure out the overall profitability and value of not only specific investments but also neighborhoods and broader markets. Generally, calculating the cap rate of your multifamily property can benefit you in three ways.

Risk Level

If a multifamily investment property has a lower cap rate, it is less risky. But it might not be a worthy and profitable investment. On the other hand, a higher cap rate is a sign of higher ROI but involves higher risk. It depends on you how you find a sweet spot to balance reward and risk.

Analyzing and Screening Potential Investment

You can use cap rate as a baseline metric to compare multiple properties. It could be your first step to investigate new investments in multifamily properties.

ROI Calculation

One of the main benefits of cap rates for a multifamily investment property is that it projects ROI (return-on-investment) in the best possible way using available data.

What is an Ideal Cap Rate for Multifamily Investments?

Did you know multifamily buildings have the lowest cap rates compared to other property asset types because of their lower risk?

Experts consider a 4 percent to 10 percent cap rate ideal for multifamily investments. But it is not as simple as it sounds. It is important to take three factors into account to compare cap rates. These include class, location, and asset type.

- **Asset Type and Cap Rate**

Cap rates can vary depending on how you evaluate your property. It might be because of the perceived risk between the asset types. As multifamily properties typically have the lowest cap rates, they also have low financial risks.

The latest survey of CBRE shows that the average cap rate for American multifamily buildings can range from 5.2 percent to 5.4 percent. However, it depends on location.

- **Asset Class and Cap Rate**

The asset class is another crucial metric to compare properties that have the same value as others based on their age, and integrity. Here is a general breakdown of multifamily asset classes;

- Class A: Less than 10 years
- Class B: 10 to 20 years old

- Class C: 20 to 30 years
- Class D: 30+ years

Apartment buildings that are newly constructed come with higher property value and less risk. This is the reason why class A multifamily buildings have significantly the lowest cap rates. While the age of the property is one factor that impacts asset class, it is the easiest way you can grade the investment when comparing the rates.

- ***Location and Cap Rate***

Real estate investors often look for ways to broaden their investment portfolio with multifamily investments. However, determining the good cap rate for the housing market can make a huge difference.

In this regard, CBRE has released a bi-annual cap-rate survey to rank ideal markets for investing in multifamily properties in the USA.

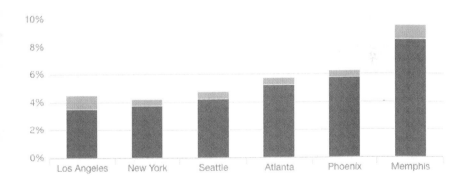

Source: https://www.cbre.us/research-and-reports/

In short, cap rate is used to find the return rate on real estate. It is more common for commercial properties, including warehouses, hotels, and office buildings. But it doesn't mean that you can't use it for multifamily residential property.

You can work out the cap rate for your investment property by subtracting the net operating income and dividing it by the market value of the property. You may also use the expected price of the property instead of its market value.

Keep in mind that only calculating the cap rate isn't enough to estimate the profit your multifamily property will generate. It is important to consider value appreciation, tax breaks, and NOI boosts.

Before you invest in multifamily real estate, consider the following things.

The Location

Purchasing a multifamily investment property starts with choosing a good location. The more attractive your location is, the higher the vacancy rate will be. You need to ensure that your multifamily complex is closer to mainstream markets, malls, and facilities, like schools and restaurants.

It is better to hire a professional for this job who knows about the city as well as the thriving real estate market. The experts can identify the well-off and prosperous neighborhoods that may work best for your multifamily real estate business.

The Total Number of Units

Building a successful multifamily business requires you to come up with the most effective business plan. When you're investing in a multifamily property, be sure the asset includes at least 20 to 30 units to maximize occupancy. The more units your apartment complex has, the better your income stream will be.

Also, it should have a good mix of units. Apartments can be of different sizes and range from an efficient apartment and 2-bedroom apartment to a 4-bedroom apartment. This ratio of the apartment is your unit mix.

So if you buy a building with 20 two-bedroom apartments and 20 one-bedroom apartments, the unit mix will be 1:1.

Potential Income

Determine the profit your multifamily property will earn. If you're a first-time investor, use helpful platforms such as Craigslist and Rentometer to determine rental income and prices. Investing in multifamily requires due diligence on your part.

Costs

When financing your multifamily real estate business, situations may vary. You have a choice to live in one apartment while renting others. This is an easy way to obtain financing for an owner-occupied property.

You can factor the income of your second unit into the lender's ratio. Make sure you know your credit scores can affect your financing options. If your credit score is not good, it will have a negative impact and make qualifying for the loan more difficult.

These three components are essential for all lenders:

- Debt-to-income ratio
- Credit scores
- Down payment

The Seller

The "seller" of a multifamily property is another important aspect you must consider before investing. It has a great impact on the price range as it partly depends on the motivation and preference of the property seller. That is why you must have a good understanding of the person you're dealing with.

Buying bank-owned property is different from investing in for-sale-by-owner properties.

Everything from requirements to the selling process is different. So, if you know how to deal with sellers, you can save money.

CHAPTER 6
MAINTAINING MULTIFAMILY RENTAL PROPERTY

Business owners can easily start with little money in the multifamily real estate business. That means you can use many ways to get your business off the ground and generate profits. However, you must understand that the profits and revenues rely on the investor's ability to manage investments.

To manage investment properties, real estate managers must consider the scope of work and prepare a to-do list. It is an effective strategy for streamlining operations and improving the property's value. This will increase income and reduce expenses.

We have discussed a few stages to help real estate investors manage their investments.

Start Small

It is always safe to start small when investing in a multifamily real estate business. That means you need to find a way to make income from the units. For example, you can buy and shift into a multi-unit building, such as a duplex, and use all the extra units as rental apartments for additional income.

It can become even more beneficial if you start by applying for owner-occupant financing to make the purchase.

Get Familiar with Basic Professional Property Management Systems

Fund managers or professional services can be a great resource to help real estate investors manage their investments. You can consult them to understand the basic property management systems that may include finding potential tenants, dealing with maintenance issues, and following state laws.

You can also use the latest property management software to find better opportunities to invest and handle various tasks, such as tenant acquisition, rent collection, and property maintenance.

Add Perks

Once you have bought the property, it is time to evaluate its condition. If it's not been looked after properly, it is hard to transform it into an income-generating property. Keep in mind that your aim is to present your multifamily building complex in the best condition. Only a well-maintained property attracts qualified and attractive tenants.

You can make improvements and add features such as lighting, HVAC, or a pool to enhance the appeal of your multifamily property. It can also help you advertise the property if you hire a professional photographer or videographer to showcase it.

Set Community Rules

It is not easy to manage multiple tenants living together in an apartment complex. Conflicts and disagreements may arise as families engage with each other. While some tenants might like having noisy parties, others may enjoy living in a peaceful and quiet environment. Some may have pets that can be dangerous to neighbors' kids.

How to deal with that?

You must establish some community rules for your multifamily property units. Make them a part of your tenancy contract, and be sure all residents adhere to these rules

Select the Right Tenants

Once your rental units are ready for new occupants, it is the right time to look for a tenant. Choosing tenants requires vigilance. You need a reliable person who can pay rent on time.

Moreover, ensure that you collect reliable references to verify your tenant's credentials. Find out about their work and family background before renting out your space. Once you are satisfied, discuss your concerns (if any) and negotiate on the security deposit. Most importantly, decide on a fixed payment schedule.

Here are some questions you should ask your tenants:

- **What are you moving to a new place?** – The expected answer could be changing jobs or the requirement to have more space.

- **How much do you earn monthly?** - The answer will give you an idea of the financial condition of your potential tenants

- **Have you ever been evicted in the past?** If you get "yes" from the candidate, do more research.

- **Do you mind if I perform a credit/background check?** If a candidate isn't comfortable with this, it is a red flag

Using Preventative Property Maintenance

Maintain Your Multifamily Property Regularly

Multifamily properties have several units to maintain. The only way to keep your tenants happy, comfortable, and satisfied is to make sure that all the units are being monitored. It requires you to be vigilant about repairing structural damages, removing pest infestation, and removing mold.

You can divide the task into four inspection steps:

- **Move-in inspection** - Do it before a new tenant moves in

- **Move-out inspection** - Do it after a tenants shifts to a new place to check the condition

- **Drive-by inspection** - It refers to a quick property evaluation from the outside

- **Seasonal inspection** - It includes seasonal tasks, such as gutter cleaning, snow removal, and tree pruning

Tracking Property Maintenance Data for Each Multifamily Unit

The best way to determine whether each unit is in a habitable condition is to maintain property maintenance data for each unit. Use software to organize and manage maintenance schedules and help you stay on top of repair and renovation tasks.

Get Familiar with Your Region's Property Management Laws

Property management laws vary from state to state. Failing to adhere to the regulation of your state may result in business dissolution, fines, and numerous federal sanctions.

Therefore, you must be familiar with the regulations. So make sure you talk to your attorney to learn how you can provide better property maintenance.

Install Energy-Efficient Lights

This tip is great for reducing the cost of your rental property. You may find energy-efficient LED lights and refrigerators expensive, but they will save you a lot in the long run. Plus, you can be more environmentally conscious.

Have a Good Property Management Marketing Plan

Multifamily property management greatly relies on a well-planned marketing strategy. If you don't use an effective advertising campaign for your multifamily building, you won't be able to entice potential tenants. As most tenants start their search from property listing sites, you need to list your multifamily building on these sites.

Many people rely on MLS (Multiple Listing Service) for finding good investment properties. The MLS is a database used by licensed real estate brokers to assist buyers and sellers with the transference of ownership of real property.

It is used to market properties based on contractual agreements made between brokers and sellers. Properties listed on the open market that meet the criteria of a good investment will be preferred. This is where having an investor-friendly real estate agent or realtor will be important if you want to succeed.

Include attractive photos of your property that make your investment property visible from every angle. You may also use social media platforms, such as Facebook, Instagram, or Twitter, to market your multifamily property. Reaching potential renters using flyers, magazines, and newspapers can also be a good idea.

Work with a Team

Managing a multifamily property is a demanding task. Consider working with a team that has a property manager, attorney, and leasing agent to deal with different issues. Your tenants can contact the assistants for inquiries.

While hiring professionals to manage your property investments is a good idea, it is crucial to supervise them. You need to oversee how they are implementing strategies and if they are suitable for your real estate or not.

What Else is needed to boost the returns of your multifamily property?

Focus on Effective Tactics of Real Estate Marketing

The multifamily real estate market has seen an interesting shift over the past couple of years. The National Association of Realtors NAR membership has hit an all-time high with 1, 3757,000 realtors before dramatically dropping with the financial housing crisis.

After hitting rock bottom with 999,000 members, it is now steadily increasing. It reached 1,100,000 members last year.

The purpose of looking over these statistics is to highlight how competition among real estate agents is heating up and is pretty fierce. That means you need some exceptional marketing skills (be it online or offline) if you really want to set your multifamily real estate business apart from the rest.

Here it's important to understand that some potential tenants and buyers now rely only on real estate agents. But most of them do a lot of leg work themselves before involving real estate experts.

Many multifamily tenants begin house quests with the internet before they approach a realtor. This is what drives the vital need for an active online and offline presence. This means if you're not engaging, active, or networking online, you're may miss out on something!

We cover a list of some tactics you should consider adding to your multifamily real estate marketing business to boost its profitability. Enumerated here are some ideas to help you rock your marketing game.

Make an Impact with Events

Successful real estate agents know that parties or events can drive buyers to you. No matter if you're a newbie in the multifamily real estate business, hosting a house warming party is an easy way to find or attract buyers.

If hosting a small get to gather doesn't appeal to you, hold a house-hunt seminar or an open house to promote your multifamily building. Also, you can host a grand neighborhood event and invite all the residents. This way, you will be able to establish and expand a social network and meet your competitors in your neighborhood.

Other convenient ways are to collect RSVPs mentioned on invitation cards to reach more people. You can even use your email addresses to saddle up your marketing ads. Leave your prospective tenants a trail of ads.

If they attend your house warming event, you can send emails to them detailing your multifamily properties and their features.

Focus on Content Creation

If you really want to stand out among multifamily real estate marketers, you may need to explore every possible niche related to it.

To do this, you have to ensure a powerful online presence and an awesome website, update blog posts, interesting videos, or Infographics. Make a high-quality video covering the best aspect and accomplishments of your multifamily real estate business.

Use bitable (a DIY video-making platform) to help you establish a strong brand presence. You may feature local landmarks to make it targeted and unique.

Moreover, use platforms like Upwork to post blogs about your niche. Make your website SEO-friendly by finding how tenants and buyers search you online. Make sure you know the Google algorithm to find out its criteria to rate your website.

List all the hotspots, referrals, and backlinks to provide easy access to your users. Also, share them on social media.

Leverage Digital Platforms

Email marketing is undoubtedly one of the most effective strategies for building a strong client relationship. Sending community-focused email newsletters to your subscribers will give your multifamily real estate business a boost.

You can notify them about the vacant units, new amenities, and services you'll offer in the nearby area. A free marketing automation platform like MailChimp can help you share ad campaigns and emails with customers and interested parties.

Build Your networking and Reputation Marketing

Expanding your network is one way to let people know what you do. Marketing can play an important role in accomplishing that reputation.

How about subscribing to HARO- Help a Reporter Out? It is a free daily email service that carries the journalist's request for expert opinions. Plus, you can join the B2B community to bring your prospects together and let them engage in a healthy business discussion.

Real estate reporters may help you get featured in the local newspaper so that you can create a positive image of your business.

Send them souvenirs with topic lists you think you should talk about with the customers. One way to reach out to the press reporters is to participate in charity events that they are covering. In short, you need to show persistence to excel in reputation marketing for your multifamily real estate business.

Saddle up Advertising

Try the paid advertisements on Facebook or Instagram. With this organic reach, you can be seen on many social networks. Facebook is very popular for its targeting features and can ensure that your multifamily real estate business is noticed. Similarly, placing Google display ads on the relevant sites can get you potential buyers.

Moreover, broadcasting on the radio will help you localize in the area and also save a lot of money. You can also give a try to Podcasts, which is a convenient way to reach the targeted audience and know their interests.

Traditional Marketing

Never underestimate the significance of print marketing. Search through a local expert directory, contact them, convince them and ask these experts to share their customer email address to contact them. Besides this, murals, billboards, and park benches are options for traditional marketing for the multifamily real estate business.

Social Media Marketing

You can promote your multifamily real estate business by sharing updates, event announcements, links, videos, and exciting contests on social media for potential tenants and buyers. By tagging businesses and important realtors, you can multiply the number of followers within seconds.

So make sure that you promote all your marketing efforts on social media.

Offline Marketing Tactics for Multifamily Real Estate Business

Multifamily real estate is more about buyers and tenants and less about just trading properties. That means to leave an impression on your prospective renter and buyers, you need to personalize communication with them. By saying personalizing communication, we mean making your clients feel special.

One great way to establish rapport & "flow" with your clients is with weekly value-added emails, FB messenger bots, SMS, social media posts, etc. In addition to that, you can incorporate strategies that can help you enhance your lead-nurturing techniques.

Check out the given list to add useful items to your strategy toolkit.

Stay Connected to your Existing Customers

As per current statistics of MarketingMetrics.com, real estate agents have a better chance of making a deal with their existing customers (70%) than they have with new prospects.

Consequently, it's important to work on the database at least two days a week to contact your existing customers.

You can work backward to review tenants' information starting from the current month. This way, you can easily begin this process of contacting and nurturing and establishing communication with existing tenants.

Entice Your Past Tenants or Buyer Back to Business

A good warm-up call or a handwritten thank you postcard can do the job. Once you have reignited your connection with the past tenants, make sure to continue this engagement strategy with some consistent communication calls and emails to keep the relationship warm.

The best way to do that is to set up a calendar. It will help you remind when to contact your buyers once a month. Offer reports, coupons, or some inexpensive freebies to win their interest.

Be Visible in Your Real Estate Community

What about setting up charity events for your town and community?

Whether it is in the form of Thanksgiving dinner, holiday drives, or a warm-up party, you have to try these methods to have your name engraved in the minds of your existing and prospective tenants and buyers.

Remember that you need to make efforts to stay fresh on their minds and have them thinking of you, especially when it's time to buy/sell a home. Your current customers are your very best source of referrals, so give them the time and attention they deserve.

Customized and personalized messages are preferred; however, value to customers can be added in a variety of ways, such as:

- Tickets and giveaways

- Coupons/gift certificates
- Local event calendars (sports, entertainment, etc.)
- Upcoming relevant real estate classes & events
- Neighborhood statistics & locator maps
- Real estate investment info
- Financing and refinancing info

Find Your Unique Value Propositions

Don't settle for offering standard real estate services. You don't have to deal with "constantly being asked to lower your commission rate".

You need to stand out from your competition by offering differentiated custom services that are beyond the ordinary to truly earn your commission and make it a no-brainer for people to choose you for rent or buy a multifamily property.

Something as simple as "Excellent Service" - Some of the biggest complaints about their property owner from tenants and buyers are the lack of communication.

So what is the key problem here?

To become a successful multifamily real estate business that stays on the mind of the clients, you must define the features and characteristics that make you unique. Tell your prospective tenants how the unique features of your multifamily property can benefit them.

Precisely, it is your unique value proposition that will set you apart from the crowd. It is something that showcases how your service is different and better than other businesses working in the same market.

Your value proposition is the key to your marketing strategy in the multifamily real estate industry. In other words, with a clear and concise value proposition, you can secure and better more business opportunities.

Follow these ideas to improve your multifamily real estate business's value proposition.

Try:

- **Drone Video Footage of Your Apartment Building -** This can be a unique approach to your marketing strategy, as it will help you increase sales in your multifamily real estate business. Team up with a high-quality videographer (3DRoomScapes) to showcase the property you're selling creatively.

- **Aerial Drone Photography -** You can win over potential tenants/ buyers and create a great impression through aerial drone photography. Add eye-catching imagery to attract and impress prospective tenants.

- **Virtual Tours -** Aerial drones are great for capturing a virtual tour. Adding voiceovers and music can please the prospective tenants/buyers. Moreover, you can enhance your internet listings with virtual tours and high-def professional photos.

FINAL VERDICT

Success doesn't happen overnight and usually requires you're a huge chunk of your time and painful trial and error. You must also have the determination to overcome several obstacles along the way and build a strong presence in the marketplace.

If you're looking for a partner that can help you through the long and arduous path, making you realize that there is no ceiling on your income in the multifamily real estate market, this **BOOK** can definitely help you!

Investing in a multifamily property has become a popular strategy, and you can use it to increase your income and diversify your investment portfolio. It is great for paying down debts and making money even during an economic crisis.

In other words, there can be numerous motives for investment, but it is essential to mull over your options before you make the decision. From knowing the right strategies to invest in multifamily, analyzing it, and applying powerful methods, to meeting maintenance requirements, you need to weigh all your options, benefits, and responsibilities before investing.

Researching rental income in your region is one of the vital considerations before renting out your units. To get benefits from your extra income, it is important to research rental income. It will help you determine the current rental rates of properties similar to yours.

It is better to explore the reasonable level of rent that your property can fetch at the beginning of the process. Otherwise, you may regret renting your multi-apartment building for a lower amount than what you can get. If you find it difficult, hiring a property manager to tackle all these matters is a safe option.

Make sure you employ an effective and comprehensive plan such as Stack. It is a tried and tested plan that can help you expand your multifamily real estate investment business. When used the right way, the method can help you reap tons of multifamily investing benefits, such as better cash flow, extensive tenants' pool, and tax benefits.

Rental income from your multifamily property not only diversifies your portfolio but also multiplies it. The rent you get from your rental property also has tax benefits, so it is worth discussing with your property manager. As a landlord, you should have enough knowledge of tax implications and deductibles.

If it is your first time and you have not invested in a multifamily property before, you must determine the ongoing cost of your property. Moreover, property maintenance and repair are also your responsibility. You require safety licenses and certificates to ensure your property is safe for the new occupants. Your property manager can best guide you in terms of legal requirements.

Also, keep in mind that buying a multifamily property may seem an easy task. However, it may become a nightmare if you are unaware of the legal requirements, state ordinances, tax laws, and property rules.

You must abide by the rules and take care of legal matters. If you find this all stressful, you can avail the services of property management companies. Working as a third party, they handle the day-to-day activities of property investors professionally. They find and screen tenants, set, adjust, and collect rent, improve cash flow, handle leases, emergencies, security deposits, maintenance, repair, and much more.

Also, investing in a multifamily property requires you to know the important landlord tenants' laws. It is not about knowing how much deposit your tenant owes you, but it is more about your responsibilities as a property owner. Your agreement must include information about electricity or gas services also. Install safety and energy-efficient lighting and power outlets.

Legal regulations may vary from state to state. For example, if you are a California resident, you must have some specific information regarding land-lord tenants' and property management laws. Ask your attorney to help you with the tenant and landlord regulations and explain government multifamily property rules to protect your rights.

Once your multifamily property is ready for new occupants, look for the best tenants. Choosing tenants is a complex process and requires vigilance. You need reliable tenants who pay timely rent and keep your property in a good condition

Rent the units only when you have all the essential information about the tenants. You need to educate your clients about the rules and what may happen if they fail to meet them.

As a multifamily investor knowing all legal matters or finding good tenants is not enough. It takes more than that when it comes to planning a long-term strategy. Put simply, what if you need to sell your property right after two months for some financial reason? You cannot evict your tenants just because it is in your best interest.

Never underestimate the importance of incorporating smart marketing tactics to promote your multifamily investment business. Promoting your business through online and offline tactics is a great way to influence the minds of your buyers and tenants.

Trust us; it is one of the best strategies to elevate a customer attraction mindset. Know that if you want to attract ideal potential clients, you need to build a mindset that supports your business instead of draining you. Focusing on customers and changing your mindset means that you need to identify thoughts that encourage you and support you.

With the right details, tips, ideas, and insights, you could replace the ups and downs of the never-ending roller coaster ride, the panic, worry, and fear that you experience in your investment business. The ideas can help you with a steady stream of appointments, more deals to close, and a confident and ambitious outlook on your business affairs.

As mentioned above, what you think has a strong effect on attracting clients. You may start building a positive mindset by reinforcing thoughts on "how well you are helping your buyers and how you are growing your multifamily business to fulfill the purpose you have." The reinforcing thoughts about "why you need to grow a prosperous business" are great to help serve the clients in a better way.

You need to consider several other things to advance for your multifamily real estate business, such as property values, price trends, nearby constructions, and local community demographics.

Things can get a little more complex, especially if you are a multifamily real estate investor. You have to deal with many properties, their maintenance, repair, and so many other things. There are ways you can deal with it smartly. Your property manager can be your go-to person if you want a smooth transition and avoid the hassle of renting out on your own.

Overall, your time is a very valuable thing. Don't waste your non-leisure, working hours doing back-end burdensome chores like repairs finding tenants and other property management tasks, etc. Instead, consider working with a team that can systemize your multifamily real estate business operations to help you focus on closing more deals.

This whole book is essentially about getting into multifamily real estate landscape and focusing on the tasks that will make you the most money in the least amount of time.

In this regard, the information mentioned above covers the important aspects you need to consider before investing in an apartment building. The book includes all the important aspects related to multifamily real estate investment that it PROMISED. It tells you everything about investing in multifamily business and easy and practical strategies to do that.

The main **TAKEAWAYS** of this book include:

- What is a multifamily business?

- How it is different from investing in a single-family home

- Why investing in a multifamily real estate business could be the best idea

- The best method to invest in a multifamily real estate business and expand it within five years

- Best investing strategies to make the multifamily business a success

- Things you must consider when investing in a multifamily real estate business

Happy Investing!

Made in the USA
Coppell, TX
26 November 2022

87126988R00079